IMAGES
of America

REMEMBERING
NORTH CAROLINA'S
CONFEDERATES

Copyright 1905 by the Rotograph Co

A 12205 Confederate Monument, Raleigh, N. C

There are two large cannons on each side of this monument in Raleigh. The inscription reads: "32 Pounder . . . taken in June 1861 when the Navy Yard at Norfolk was abandoned by the United States. Banded and converted, at Richmond into a 6 inch rifle—Mounted at Fort Caswell, North Carolina. Dismounted by exploding magazines, when the Confederates evacuated that Fort in January 1865." The cannons were presented to the state by the U.S. War Department in 1902. (Hardy.)

ON THE COVER: Following Reconstruction, old soldiers all across the South began to gather in reunions with fellow comrades who had followed the starry cross from 1861 until 1865. They met in local reunions, like the one pictured here in Asheville, Buncombe County; in statewide reunions; and in national reunions. This reunion took place on July 4, 1889, at the home of James M. Ray, 60th North Carolina Troops. (DRM.)

IMAGES
of America

REMEMBERING
NORTH CAROLINA'S
CONFEDERATES

Michael C. Hardy

ARCADIA
PUBLISHING

Published by Arcadia Publishing
Charleston, South Carolina

Printed in the United States of America

Library of Congress Catalog Card Number: 2006924927

For all general information contact Arcadia Publishing at:
Telephone 843-853-2070
Fax 843-853-0044
E-mail sales@arcadiapublishing.com
For customer service and orders:
Toll-Free 1-888-313-2665

Visit us on the Internet at www.arcadiapublishing.com

To the 125,000 Confederate soldiers who served from North Carolina in the Confederate army and navy during the War Between the States— "he fought a good fight and has left a record of which we, his surviving comrades, are proud and which is a heritage of glory to his family, and his descendants."
—"Burial Ritual for Veterans" Confederate Veteran, 1895

CONTENTS

ACKNOWLEDGMENTS

In the next 128 pages, one finds but a sampling of images from across the Old North State—not every photograph of a battle-scared veteran, nor gathering of old soldiers, nor monument erected to the honored dead, nor every chiseled stone is presented, only a selection of such images. There are many, many more photographs waiting to be found.

The author would especially like to thank his darling wife, Elizabeth Baird Hardy.

Librarians, archivists, and keepers of family history across the state contributed to this volume. Without these folks, this project would have not been possible. The sources of images found scattered throughout this volume include the following: Donald and Gloria Archer (Archer); Cabarrus County Public Library (Cabarrus); Caldwell County Historical Museum (Caldwell); University of North Carolina at Charlotte (Charlotte); Chatham County Historical Association (Chatham); Jeff Cordell (Cordell); Harold Dagenhart (Dagenhart); Dry Ridge Museum (DRM); Dave Edwards (Edwards); Forsyth County Public Library (Forsyth); Edward Harding (Harding); Michael C. Hardy (Hardy); Lower Cape Fear Historical Society (Cape Fear); National Park Service (NPS); NC Collection, Pack Memorial Library, Asheville (Pack); North Carolina Department of Archives and History (SA); North Carolina Museum of History (SM); Richmond County Historical Society (Richmond); and Jane McCrary Collection, Roswell Bosse History Room, Transylvania County Library Archives (Transylvania).

Following the end of Reconstruction, soldiers started to gather in formal reunions, like this one in Asheville. These reunions were held all across the South in local communities. Many states held a statewide reunion once a year. National reunions were also held once a year in large Southern cities like New Orleans, Richmond, or Chattanooga. (Pack.)

INTRODUCTION

"First at Bethel, farthest to the front at Gettysburg and Chickamauga, and last at Appomattox." For over a century, this quote has proclaimed North Carolina's role during the War for Southern Independence. North Carolina sent over 125,000 men in more than 70 regiments into the Confederate army. The first land battle of the war, fought at Big Bethel, Virginia, on June 10, 1861, was a battle involving mostly North Carolina soldiers; a Tar Heel man, Henry Wyatt of Company A, 1st North Carolina Volunteers, was killed, the first battlefield fatality of the war.

North Carolinians were at the forefront of many important battles. Who can forget the story of Anderson's North Carolina brigade in the Sunken Road at Sharpsburg, or the heroic deeds of the 26th North Carolina at Gettysburg, or the 58th North Carolina at Chickamauga, or the 37th North Carolina at Spotsylvania Court House? At Appomattox, portions of the 4th and 14th North Carolina Troops fired the last volley in Virginia.

The contributions at home were just as great. Foodstuffs, clothing, and other munitions of war all were manufactured within the state or came through the blockade, at times on a state-owned blockade runner. Not only did North Carolina supply her own troops, but she provided much-needed items for men from other states as well. The hand of war also touched the very soil of the Old North State. From the raid by women on commissary stores in Burnsville in Yancey County and the skirmish on Beech Mountain in Watauga County, to the struggle between Joe Johnston and William Sherman at Bentonville and the capitulation of Fort Fisher near Wilmington, events that took place in North Carolina touched the lives of the people who lived here and all across the Confederacy.

In April and May 1865, the war ended. North Carolina had supplied one fifth of all soldiers who served under the Stars and Bars. Out of the 125,000 or more Tar Heel men who served, 40,275 died, either on the battlefield, in camp, in hospitals, or in Northern prison camps. And the deaths among the civilian population will always be unknown.

A year later, a group of ladies met in Raleigh. Led by Nancy Branch, the widow of Gen. Lawrence Branch, they formed the Ladies Memorial Association of Wake County. The goals of the group were to "protect and care for the graves of our Confederate soldiers." On May 10, 1867, the anniversary of the death of Thomas J. "Stonewall" Jackson, a decoration day was held at the Oakwood Cemetery in Raleigh. In the months and years following the war, during Reconstruction, men were forbidden to meet in large groups, and other memorial groups made up of ladies (with men as helpers) sprang up across the state and began to honor the fallen Confederate soldier. Small monuments appeared in cemeteries, starting with the Cross Creek Cemetery in Fayetteville in 1868.

By the late 1870s, the days of the Radical Republican rule and Reconstruction had started to wane. The veterans themselves started getting together, and in October 1881, North Carolina's Society of Ex-Confederate Soldiers and Sailors was organized. Other organizations in other states were also created, and in 1881, the national United Confederate Veterans (UCV) was organized. Maj. Gen. John B. Gordon was the first commander.

A North Carolina division of the UCV was placed over all of the chapters, or "camps," in the state. By 1901, there were 70 North Carolina camps. Many of the camps were named in honor of a Confederate soldier from the area, like the Nimrod Triplett Camp (1273) in Boone. Triplett, a member of Company D, 1st North Carolina Cavalry, was killed during the war. Other camps chose geographic features to distinguish themselves; the Wilmington Camp was known as the Cape Fear Camp (254). Besides a name, each camp was also given a number.

Each camp normally held a reunion once a year and sent delegates to statewide or national reunions. The first national reunion was held in Chattanooga, Tennessee, July 3–5, 1890. Former Confederate major general John B. Gordon was the first commander of the national organization. Many of the major cities in the South, including Charlotte in 1930, also hosted reunions.

Another organization sprang up along with the UCV: the United Daughters of the Confederacy (UDC). Many of the ladies' memorial associations and other supplementary societies organized themselves into a national organization in Nashville, Tennessee, in September 1894. The UDC began in earnest to commemorate the common Confederate soldier. Many of the wonderful monuments that grace the courthouse squares across the South can be traced to the work of the UDC.

The veterans' reunions and monument dedications peaked in the 1910s and 1920s. There were at least 50 monuments or markers dedicated in those two decades in the Tar Heel State, not to mention monuments to North Carolina soldiers in Vicksburg, Mississippi; Appomattox, Virginia; and Gettysburg, Pennsylvania. With the passing of time, there were fewer and fewer veterans alive or physically able to make their way to the gatherings. North Carolina's last Confederate soldier, Sam Bennett, died in his native Yancey County on March 8, 1951, two months before his 101st birthday. Today the UDC, and another organization, the Sons of Confederate Veterans, continue the work of erecting monuments and perpetuating the memory of the Confederate soldier from North Carolina.

Within these pages, one will find a glimpse of the commemorations that have occupied our cultural landscape for the past 145 years. From the photographs of the veterans with their tattered banners, to postcards showing the monuments our ancestors erected to their memory, to the tombstones and grave markers that recalled their service, this book, like the events and monuments it captures, is a brief attempt to remember North Carolina's Confederate soldiers.

One

THE MOUNTAINS

Western North Carolina was quick to organize companies for the defense of the state. Even before the state left the Union, companies like the Watauga Troopers of Watauga County, the Black Mountain Boys from Yancey County, and the Rough and Ready Guards of Buncombe County had formed and were on their way to offer their services to the state. Western North Carolina continued to provide men throughout the war. At one point, Yancey County passed a resolution saying that there were no more men to send. But as the war progressed, it took a different face in the mountains. The war truly became a Civil War. And in no place was the cliché of "brother against brother" more true than in the mountains. Not only did the mountains provide safe havens for bands of deserters from both sides, conscript dodgers, rogues, and bushwhackers, but in many communities, family members turned on each other. While the war formally ended in April and May 1865, these misunderstandings and ill feelings between and within families often lasted for generations.

Some in Western North Carolina wanted to remember their service to the Confederacy during the war. There were United Confederate Veteran camps and United Daughters of the Confederacy chapters in a few towns. In towns without veteran organizations, the veterans themselves would often travel to cities where reunions were taking place. But there are by far fewer monuments to Confederate soldiers in Western North Carolina in comparison to other areas of the state. And outside of Waynesville and Asheville, there are no cemeteries containing large numbers of Confederate dead.

L-18   VIEW OF THE SQUARE, LENOIR, N. C.

SHOWING CONFEDERATE MONUMENT AND CALDWELL COUNTY HOUSE

Dedicated on June 3, 1910, the monument in Lenoir, Caldwell County, is 35 feet high and constructed of granite. There were an estimated 6,000 people present during the unveiling, including Justice Walter Clark. On the sides are a furled Confederate flag, the companies from Caldwell County, and a portion of Theodore O'Hara's poem, "Bivouac of the Dead." In 1964, the monument was moved out of the center of the street to a position beside the courthouse. (Hardy.)

Known today as Connemara, this *c.* 1839 Greek Revival summer house was constructed by Christopher Memminger. Born in Germany, he represented South Carolina, the Palmetto State, in the Confederate Congress and then served as secretary of the treasury for Jefferson Davis. The house was purchased in 1945 by Carl Sandburg, the author of the Pulitzer Prize–winning *Lincoln*. Today the site is a National Historic Site. (Hardy.)

On September 26, 1922, a large number of veterans gathered at the Grove Park Inn, a popular resort in Asheville, Buncombe County, North Carolina. Many of the veterans can be seen wearing iron crosses and reunion ribbons. They were photographed by H. W. Pelton. (Pack.)

Harvey Davis was born in Catawba County, North Carolina, on July 17, 1840. He was living in Watauga County when he enlisted in Company D, 1st North Carolina Cavalry, and was mustered in as a private. Davis was wounded in the left elbow on September 22, 1863, and retired to the Invalid Corps on May 7, 1864. He survived the war and died on December 29, 1932. Davis is buried in the Old Bethany Lutheran Cemetery in Watauga County. (Hardy.)

This group of veterans gathered in Brevard, Franklin County, on an unknown date. Shown from left to right are (first row) Marcus Case, Mass Kukyendahl, Charles Osborne, Felix Rabb, Robert Bryson, unidentified, and James Wilson; (second row) Lewis Summay, Ephriam Clayton, Matt Neely, ? Fisher, William Osborne, David England, Thomas Galloway, Theodore Davidson, William Deaver, and Joseph Miller; (third row) Miles Maggie Deaver, Jasper Orr, J. M. Hamlin, Thomas Cash, and George Wilson; (fourth row) Annie Gash. (Transylvania.)

Wartime governor Zebulon Baird Vance was born on this site in northern Buncombe County in 1830. The cabin is a reconstruction based on photographs of his father's cabin and was built around the original chimney. Only one other birthplace for a North Carolina governor, Charles B. Aycock, is preserved as a state historic site. (Hardy.)

Located on the grounds of the Surry County Courthouse in Dobson is this monument to local soldiers. On the reverse of the monument are North Carolina and Confederate flags, a quote by Robert E. Lee, and the words "erected by Sons of Confederate Veterans Camp 1598 May 20, 2000." (Hardy.)

Born in Burke County in 1844, James Steward was a member of Company B, 58th North Carolina Troops (NCT). His hearing was damaged by a shell during the Battle of Chickamauga in September 1863. He lies buried under a government-issued stone in the Pineola Presbyterian Church in Avery County. (Hardy.)

The Rough and Ready Guards, which became Company F, 14th North Carolina Troops, gather for a reunion after the war with their former captain, Zebulon B. Vance. The reunion took place at Vance's mountain home, Gombroom, near Black Mountain. Vance commanded the company from May 3, 1861, until August 27, 1861, when he was elected colonel of the 26th North Carolina Troops. The 14th North Carolina was a component of Ramseur's Brigade, and it helped save the Army of Northern Virginia on May 12, 1864, at Spotsylvania Court House in Virginia. Pictured are, from left to right, William Grudger, James Smith, Perry Gaston, William Garrison, Riley Powers, Zebulon Vance, David Grudger, unidentified, Alfred Walton, J. J. Smith, unidentified, Jim Hughes, Caney Allison, Jesse Green, James Grudger, Wesley Hicks (the company cook), Gay Williams, Thomas Brooks, Vic Baird, Alfred Stevens, Andy Hunter, and Billy Hunter. (Pack.)

John H. Waggoner's tombstone, located in the Roaring Creek Cemetery in Ashe County, proudly bears Waggoner's service to the Confederacy. But his service record tells a different story. Private Waggoner enlisted in Company A, 34th NCT on August 10, 1861. He was mustered in as a musician, was wounded on June 27, 1862, and was dropped from the rolls of the company prior to September 1, 1863, for desertion. (Hardy.)

Erected in 1909, the Macon County monument, located across from the courthouse, is constructed of Georgia marble and topped with a marble Confederate soldier carved in Italy. There were seven companies of infantry and cavalry to come from Macon County during the war: Company C, 14th North Carolina State Troops (NCST); Company A, 23rd NCT; Company K, 26th NCT; Company B, 31st NCT; Companies H, I, and K, 43rd NCT; and Company A, 59th NCT. (Hardy.)

Here a group of veterans gather in Watauga County. From left to right are (first row) two unidentified, Ranzey Miller, Henry Miller, Wiley Norris, unidentified, ? Farthing, unidentified, Calvin Cotrell, unidentified, Webster Davis, and Speck Henson; (second row) Sam Bishop, Elijah Norris, William Blair, William P. Coffey, ? Critcher, John Hughes, Harvey Davis, Bill Hodges, William S. Cook, Jerome Presnell, and Bill Norris. (Hardy.)

Talk of erecting a monument to Zebulon Vance, colonel of the 26th North Carolina, three-time governor, and U.S. senator, began just after his death. But it was not until May 1896 that work began. The cornerstone was laid in a public cemetery on December 22, 1897, and work was completed three months later on this monument in Pack Square in Asheville. (Pack.)

This photograph is labeled as the first Confederate reunion in Asheville. It took place on July 4, 1889, at Ramoth, the home of Lt. Col. James M. Ray of the 60th North Carolina Troops. Lt. Col. James T. Weaver is on the front right. During Reconstruction, large groups of men, including veterans, were forbidden to gather together. Once the restrictions of Reconstruction had been lifted, public meeting was again permissible, and many veterans took the opportunity to meet and reminisce whenever possible. While some old soldiers never spoke of the war or attended reunions or memorial events, others welcomed the opportunity to see old friends and celebrate their service. Veterans like Lieutenant Colonel Ray who had large homes often offered their hospitality to their former comrades. The photograph was taken by E. E. Brown of Patton Avenue of Asheville. (DRM.)

As time passed, veterans from both the Confederate and Union armies began to gather together for reunions. Here a group of veterans from both sides gathers for a reunion in Waynesville at the Haywood County Courthouse, and men who once fought on opposing sides proudly display the flags of both armies. The photograph was taken July 4, 1910. (SA.)

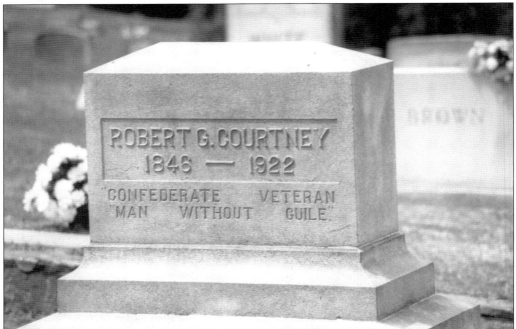

A "man without guile" is the description on the gravestone of Robert G. Courtney in the Lenoir City Cemetery in Caldwell County. Courtney served in Company C, 8th Battalion Junior Reserves. Following the war, he journeyed to California but returned to Caldwell County, where he was a businessman. (Hardy.)

Joseph Crouch, buried in the Macedonia Baptist Church Cemetery in Alexander County, enlisted in August 1862. He was wounded in the arm at Fredericksburg in December 1862 and in the leg in May 1864 at Spotsylvania, where he was captured. Private Crouch spent the rest of the war at Fort Delaware, where he was released on June 15, 1865, after taking the Oath of Allegiance. (Hardy.)

A dinner was held in honor of the attending Confederate veterans on the day that the Confederate monument in Morganton, Burke County, was dedicated. Chief Justice Walter Clark was the orator. The monument, unveiled on June 22, 1918, has a nine-foot-tall bronze soldier on a granite base with the names of local soldiers on marble tablets. (Hardy.)

ASHEVILLE

Col. James Mitchell Ray, with his sword upon his shoulder, poses with a large group of veterans who served the Confederacy in the 60th North Carolina Troops. This early reunion was possibly located at Camp Ray in Buncombe County, near Haw Creek. The 60th North Carolina was one of four North Carolina regiments to serve in the western theater of the war (the 29th, 39th, and 58th were the other regiments). Toward the end of the war, the remnants of the 60th North

Col James Mitchell Ray and veterans of his 60th North Carol
Regiment at one of the early reunions held probably at Camp
Ray near Haw Creek on what is now called the Black Mountain

Carolina were consolidated with the 58th North Carolina. Col. Washington M. Hardy, who later commanded a brigade during the Battle of Bentonville, was the regiment's colonel. A number of the veterans are wearing reunion medals or ribbons, and the flag they hold is an American flag, once the flag they fought against. (Pack.)

21

This photograph is labeled as the "last Old Soldier Reunion to be held in Alexander County . . . at Stoney Point . . . at the Pinkey Wyatt House." The date of the reunion was 1902. A remarkable number of veterans appear in the picture, at times in rows four men deep. (Dagenhart.)

Buried in the Green Hill Cemetery in Waynesville, Haywood County, John H. Mull enlisted on May 4, 1861, and served as a private in Company L, 16th North Carolina Troops (6th North Carolina Volunteers). On October 5, 1862, he was transferred to Company E, Infantry Battalion, Thomas's Legion. (Hardy.)

Governor Vance's brother, Robert Brank Vance, became colonel of the 29th North Carolina in 1861. Vance was wounded at Stones River, Tennessee, and became brigadier general on March 4, 1863. He commanded in Western North Carolina until captured at Crosby Creek, Tennessee, on January 14, 1864. Following the war, Vance was a state and congressional representative. He died November 28, 1899, and is interred in the Riverside Cemetery in Asheville. (Hardy.)

James Green Martin, known as "One Wing" due to the loss of his arm during the Mexican War, commanded the district of Western North Carolina from July 1864 until March 1865. He was born in Elizabeth City, attended West Point, and died on October 4, 1878. Martin is interred in the Riverside Cemetery in Asheville. (Hardy.)

This group of veterans is gathered at a reunion in Lenoir, Caldwell County. They proudly display small Army of Northern Virginia battle flags, and some of the old soldiers are wearing reunion medals. Men from Caldwell County served in the 22nd North Carolina, 26th North Carolina, and 58th North Carolina Regiments. (Caldwell.)

A large number of reunions, both great and small, took place in Asheville between 1915 and 1927. Here a group of gray-haired veterans and two ladies pose on the front steps and porch of the home of a Mrs. Glenn. (Pack.)

Construction on this grand Confederate monument, located in Taylorsville in Alexander County, began on June 5, 1958, and was completed a year later, on June 1, 1959. It was made possible largely through the work of Virgil "Guss" Beckham, a local attorney. Beckham hauled nearly all of the materials for this monument in his 1953 Chevrolet pickup. The monument is made of local granite and Tennessee granite, topped with a young, beardless, battle-ready Confederate infantry soldier at parade rest. On December 1, 1958, the Alexander County Commissioners voted $1,175 for the purchase of a cannon to complement the monument. The cannon, which has a plaque that denotes its service during the Battle of Gettysburg in support of the men of the Pickett-Pettigrew-Trimble charge, stands sentinel beside the monument. (Hardy.)

Most of the Cherokees were sent west by the federal government in the 1830s. Those who were able to stay behind lived on land purchased for them by William H. Thomas. When the war came, Thomas formed a group of Cherokee Indians and Highland whites, named Thomas's Legion. The eastern band of the Cherokees often met for reunions after the war, and there is even a monument to the Cherokee veterans on the reservation. (SA.)

If the label on this print, "First March," is correct, then it took place on August 27, 1891, in Blowing Rock, Watauga County. The Blowing Rock Assembly Grounds hosted numerous reunions for Confederate, and later Union, veterans. (Hardy.)

Nine Buncombe County Confederate veterans gather in this photograph, taken prior to 1923. Several of the men wear reunion ribbons and badges on their lapels. The tall, bearded gentleman holding the flag is Pvt. Robert Williams of Company F of the 14th Regiment North Carolina Troops, a company known as the "Rough and Ready Guards" and raised by future wartime governor Zebulon Baird Vance. (SA.)

One of the rising stars in the Confederate army was James Byron Gordon. The prewar merchant, farmer, and state legislator rose through the ranks of the 1st North Carolina Cavalry and, by 1862, was commanding a brigade under J. E. B. Stuart. Gordon was mortally wounded the same day as Stuart, dying in Richmond on May 18, 1864. He is buried in the St. Paul's Episcopal Church Cemetery, Wilkes County. (Hardy.)

Walter Lenoir Jones was a private in Company A, 22nd North Carolina Troops. He was mortally wounded on July 3, 1863, at Gettysburg, Pennsylvania. This stone resides beside that of his brother, Lt. Col. John T. Jones, in the Chapel of Rest Cemetery in Caldwell County. (Hardy.)

McDowell County veterans at this reunion are, from left to right, (first row) Sidney Poteat, Andrew Mode, unidentified, Jethro Morgan, unidentified, James Pyatt, Joe Swann, and unidentified; (second row) unidentified, Tom Lytle, Marion "General" Harris, unidentified, John Kanipe, Cornelius Bradley, two unidentified, Jim Morris, Andy Yount, two unidentified, Stephen Hensley, and unidentified; (third row) Lee Williams, Bill Crawford, two unidentified, and J. M. Clay; (fourth row) Captain Gardin, John Lavender, Milton Lytle, Joe Brown, two unidentified, Preacher Kaylor, Stephen Gruber, and two unidentified. (Cordell.)

Off the Blue Ridge Parkway, near mile marker 422, is the Confederate Memorial Forest. The project began in 1940, with the planting of 125,000 red spruce seedlings, one for every Tar Heel soldier. A monument was dedicated in 1956, depicted in this photograph. The forest was rededicated in 2001, but the monument seems to have disappeared. (SA.)

Between 2,000 and 3,000 people had gathered in the fall of 1887 for the "Junebug Celebration." But the train carrying many of the dignitaries derailed the night before the reunion, and the people of Alexander County "had the celebration largely to themselves." Over 200 veterans were present, and after a short address, Romulus Zachariah Linney invited his former comrades to his home for a dinner. (Dagenhart.)

William S. Cook was born in North Carolina on April 29, 1843, and lived in Watauga County. On August 5, 1862, he enlisted in Company I, 58th North Carolina Troops. Private Cook was captured near Atlanta, Georgia, on July 28, 1864, possibly after being wounded. He was incarcerated at Camp Chase, Ohio, and was exchanged in March 1865. Cook, shown here wearing his iron cross, died on March 16, 1926, and is buried in Caldwell County. (Hardy.)

Enlisting at the age of 25 on June 29, 1861, James M. Henderson served in Company F, 25th North Carolina Troops. He was wounded in a fight at Globe Tavern, Virginia, on August 21, 1864, and died of his wounds on August 21. This marker is in the Green Hill Cemetery in Waynesville, Haywood County. (Hardy.)

Many of the veterans in this photograph, published in the October 23, 1927, issue of the *Asheville Times*, are proudly wearing their United Confederate Veteran uniforms with badges and reunion ribbons. The location of the photograph is unknown but might be the Woodfin House. It is also believed that many of these veterans served in Company F, 25th North Carolina Troops. (Pack.)

It took seven years, from 1903 to 1910, for the Davis-Dickerson-Mills Chapter of the United Daughters of the Confederacy to raise the funds for the monument on the grounds of the Rutherford County Courthouse. The monument is in honor of the "Men and Women of the Confederacy" who served from Rutherford County. (Hardy.)

Among the dignitaries who attended the August 8, 1889, "Rebel Reunion" in Waynesville, Haywood County, are Gov. David G. Fowle, who is up front between two ladies, and Gen. Thomas L. Clingman, the white-haired gentlemen up front on the right. The row behind the governor includes Alphonso C. Avery, Robert B. Vance, Col. John S. McElroy, and Thomas Johnston. (Pack.)

Countless Confederate and Union soldiers occupy graves simply marked "Unknown." In the Newton Academy Cemetery in Asheville, Bumcombe County, lie the graves of several Confederate and Union soldiers. The circumstances of their deaths remain a mystery. (Hardy.)

Shelby's Confederate monument was erected on November 21, 1906, to the delight of a throng of spectators. A bronze soldier stands atop a granite base, with his rifle at the ready and his blanket roll slung over his shoulder. This monument, which stands on the Cleveland County courthouse grounds, cost $2,500 and was provided by the Cleveland Guards Chapter of the United Daughters of the Confederacy. (Hardy.)

Born in Wurtemberg in 1803, Christopher Memminger moved to the United States in 1806. He was a prewar lawyer and South Carolina legislator who had a summer home in Flat Rock, North Carolina. During the war, Memminger served as secretary of the treasury for the Confederate government. He died in Charleston and is buried at the St. John in the Wilderness Episcopal Church in Flat Rock, Henderson County. (Hardy.)

On May 3, 1890, a group of veterans gathered on the front porch of Gombroom, the home of Zebulon Vance. Gombroom was located eight miles from the railway station in Black Mountain, Bumcombe County. From left to right are (first row, with their feet on the ground) Lt. William M. Gudger, Company F, 14th NCT; Pvt. David M. Gudger, Company F, 14th NCT; Capt. James M. Gudger, Company F, 14th NCT; Lt. Gay M. Williams, Company F, 14th NCT; Billy Hunter; Vic Baird; Pvt. Thomas Hicks, Company F, 14th NCT; and Pvt. Wesley Hicks, Company I, 22nd NCT; (second row) Pvt. James M. Smith, Company F, 14th NCT; Pvt. William C. Garrison, Company F, 14th NCT; Pvt. James J. White, Company F, 14th NCT; Sgt. Noble B. Westall, Company F, 14th NCT; Cpl. Jesse M. Green, Company F, 14th NCT; and Pvt. Alfred Walton, 29th NCT; (third row) Pvt. John M. Stepp, Company H, 29th NCT; Jim Hughey; Albert Lytle; Sen. Zebulon B. Vance and his wife, Harriett; Pvt. Riley Powers, Company F, 14th NCT; Riley Pitillol; and Perry Gaston. (Pack.)

One of the more colorful characters during the Civil War was William Holland Thomas. The representative of the eastern band of the Cherokees, Thomas was both a businessman and a state senator. Thomas raised and equipped a group during the war called Thomas's Legion of Cherokee Indians and Highlanders, which fought largely in Western North Carolina. He is buried in the Green Hill Cemetery in Haywood County. (Hardy.)

William Marsh, despite being captured twice and wounded once, survived the war. He served as a private in Company A, 28th North Carolina Troops, and is buried at the Mount Hermon Baptist Church Cemetery in Surry County. The stone that marks his grave also commemorates his wartime service. (Hardy.)

This image, labeled in the bottom right corner as a "Souvenir of Veterans' Reception" was made at the home of Mrs. M. A. E. Woodbridge in Brevard on August 14, 1911, and was inscribed to Mrs. M. A. (Stonewall) Jackson. Most of the old soldiers sport badges on their lapels, and they proudly wave two Confederate flags. The pictured veterans are, from left to right, (first row) unidentified, Lewis Summay, Samuel Lance, Thomas Gash, Felix Rabb, William Aiken, Ephriam Clayton, J. M. Hamlin, and E. T. Henning; (second row) Maj. W. E. Breese, Asbury Shuford, unidentified, John Allison, Jasper Orr, unidentified, ? Aiken, unidentified, Joseph Miller, Joseph Kern, unidentified, James Wilson, William Deaver, J. M. Thrash, unidentified, and Crayton Gillespie. James Wilson, who stands just to the right of the second national flag, was wounded on the picket line at Chancellorsville at the same time as Stonewall Jackson's fateful wounding by his own troops. (Transylvania.)

Two

SOUTHERN PIEDMONT AND FOOTHILLS

The Southern Piedmont and foothill section of North Carolina was the industrial center of the state. Charlotte not only had a branch of the U.S. Mint, but also had woolen mills, flour and wheat mills, carriage manufacturers, and tanneries. Mecklenburg County supposedly supplied more men to the Confederacy than any other North Carolina county. Gaston County, to the west of Charlotte, had woolen mills (some of the largest in the state), flour and gristmills, an ironworks, and three gold mines. During the war, thousands of men from these counties joined the Confederate cause. One of the largest conscription camps in the state was located in Iredell County, and to its east, in Rowan County, was Salisbury prison, the largest structure of its kind in the state. Zebulon Vance was arrested in Salisbury after the war and sent to prison in Washington, D.C. Charlotte was the host of the 39th annual reunion of the United Confederate Veterans in 1929, the only North Carolina city to obtain such an honor. There were also Confederate hospitals in Charlotte and Salisbury, and the cemeteries in those cities have Confederate plots in their honor.

This monument stands on the courthouse grounds in Concord. The upper inscription reads: "1861 In Memoriam 1865. This monument is erected to the memory of the Confederate Dead of Cabarrus County, North Carolina." The lower inscription reads: "With granite and marble and branch of the cypress / The emblem of peace, shall thy slumbers enshrine, / Then take this memento, 'tis all we can offer / Oh! Grave of our comrade, this tribute is thine." (Hardy.)

Like so many other cities in North Carolina and across the South, Salisbury, in Rowan County, hosted its own United Confederate Veterans camp and frequently had reunions. This 1914 reunion photograph captures a large group of weathered veterans, a few of whom appear to be wearing reunion badges or ribbons. (Rowan.)

This large group of veterans gathered in Wadesboro on January 19, 1906, for the unveiling of Anson County's Confederate monument. The soldiers were presented with Crosses of Honor, and one of the addresses was made by Col. Risden T. Bennett of the 14th North Carolina, who is wearing a white suit. The man on the horse is William A. Smith, honorary United Confederate Veterans general. (Edwards.)

Many a soldier lost a limb to the surgeon's saw during the war. This one-legged veteran, Samuel Eller, enlisted in Company H, 23rd North Carolina Troops, on September 3, 1862. He was struck in the left leg "by 3 minnie balls" and captured on July 1, 1863, at Gettysburg, Pennsylvania. Eller was exchanged and transferred to the Invalid Corps on June 9, 1864. Eller continued to make Rowan County his home following the war. (SA.)

At this early-20th-century Salisbury veterans' reunion, the old soldiers are seated in chairs on a sidewalk in town. Many of the reunion photographs appear to have been shot in less urban settings and include even elderly veterans seated on the ground, but these gentlemen, many of whom are holding canes, were likely grateful for the more comfortable environment. (Rowan.)

In the wake of the federal occupation of Raleigh, Gov. Zebulon Vance moved to this house in Statesville. It was here that Vance was eating breakfast when federal troopers arrived and arrested him. It was his 35th birthday. Vance was taken to Washington, D.C., where he was incarcerated along with other Southern governors. The house was later moved to a local park. (Hardy.)

The Gaston County Confederate Monument, pictured here in an undated photograph, stands in front of the old Gaston County Courthouse, paying homage to the Confederate soldiers who served from Gaston County. The base is decorated with a partially furled flag on a broken flagpole, and the obelisk is surmounted by a slouch-hatted solider at parade rest. (SM.)

Laban Wilson Cline was 17 years old when he enlisted in Company E, 12th North Carolina State Troops, on March 10, 1864. He was wounded at least twice, possibly three times, in battle. Cline is buried in the Fairgrove United Methodist Church Cemetery, Catawba County, where this stone denotes his service. (Hardy.)

This May 30, 1903, celebration at Buffalo Presbyterian Church in Sanford, Lee County, is the United Daughters of the Confederacy Memorial Day and includes a number of ladies and children in addition to the former soldiers, one of whom is Col. Fred Olds. Participants display flags of various sizes, and a dinner is being prepared in the background. (SA.)

Charles Fisher was born in Rowan County in 1816. He attended Yale and was a planter and railroad president prior to the war. He also was editor of the *Western Carolinian* and in the North Carolina legislature. He was colonel of the 6th North Carolina State Troops and was killed on July 21, 1861, at the battle of Bull Run. He is interred in the Old Lutheran Cemetery, Rowan County. (Hardy.)

While many Confederate sections in cemeteries are exclusively for soldiers reinterred from a specific site, the section in Elmwood Cemetery, Charlotte, includes both a number of unidentified soldiers reinterred from battlefield graves as well as Confederate soldiers who are identified and died after the war. The handsome, stepped obelisk in this section bears the following inscription: "Erected by the Women of Charlotte, to the Confederate Soldiers of Mecklenburg County and The Unknown Soldiers who rest here. 1861–1865. We Honor Them and Revere Them." Also buried in this large and beautiful cemetery are two Confederate generals: Rufus Barringer and Thomas Fenwick Drayton. Barringer was a brother-in-law to both D. H. Hill and Thomas J. "Stonewall" Jackson. Both Barringer and Drayton died after the war. Col. Charles C. Lee, commander of the 37th North Carolina Troops, killed at the Battle of Seven Days, is also buried here. Elmwood is the largest cemetery in Mecklenburg County and was established in 1851. (Hardy.)

On the top of the Confederate monument in Wadesboro is a bronze statue based upon the likeness of noted Ansonville soldier Sgt. John Richardson. He served in Company A, 23rd North Carolina State Troops. The photograph here was taken on the dedication day of the monument, January 19, 1906. The inscriptions on the monument were written by Col. Risden Tyler Bennett. One inscription bears the date of the monument's installation and gives credit to the work of the Anson County Chapter (357) of the United Daughters of the Confederacy for their efforts

in getting the monument placed. Another inscription reads: "By this monument we translate our homage for the soldiers of Anson County, who served in the war between the government and the Confederate States." Over 1,300 Anson County men served in the Confederacy. Their specific companies are listed on the monument: Company C of the 14th, Company A of the 23rd, Company K of the 26th, Company B of the 31st, Companies H, I, and K of the 43rd, and Company A of the 59th North Carolina Troops. (Edwards.)

So many North Carolina soldiers who died of disease or were killed on a battlefield never made it home. Many family members sought to commemorate these soldiers in their local cemeteries. This beautifully carved marker in the Back Creek Presbyterian Church Cemetery is for Stephen A. Brown of the 14th NCT, who died of wounds on June 28, 1862, and Lt. J. H. Kistler, color-bearer of the 24th NCT, who died of wounds on May 24, 1863.

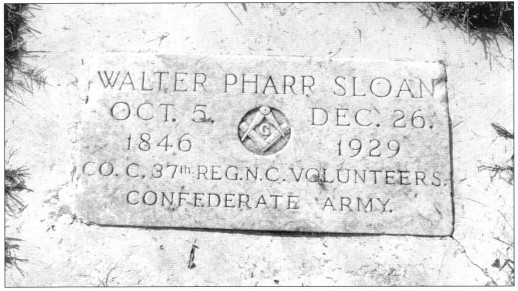

Walter Pharr Sloan served as a sergeant in Company B, 2nd Regiment of the North Carolina Junior Reserves prior to transferring to Company C, 37th North Carolina Troops. He was present from October 10, 1864, through February 1865 but did not receive a parole at Appomattox. He is buried in the Davidson College Cemetery, Mecklenburg County. (Hardy.)

The Walker brothers, Henry J. and Levi Jasper, lived in Mecklenburg County when the war began. They joined Company B, 13th North Carolina Troops (3rd North Carolina Volunteers), in May 1861. Levi lost his leg on July 1, 1863, as he carried the regiment's colors at Gettysburg, Pennsylvania. Henry was wounded on July 13, 1863, as the Army of Northern Virginia retreated from Pennsylvania. (SM.)

Maj. David Pinkney Rowe, of the 12th North Carolina State Troops, was mortally wounded on May 2, 1863, during the Battle of Chancellorsville, Virginia. Sidney H. Rowe started out the war in Company F, 23rd North Carolina Troops, but later transferred to Company A, 12th North Carolina. He died of pneumonia in prison at Elmira, New York, on December 20, 1864. This cenotaph for these two Rowe family members stands at the St. Luke's Church Cemetery in Catawba County. (Hardy.)

SALISBURY, NC

These veterans at a Salisbury reunion proudly display their United Confederate Veterans banner, which reads "Col. Chas. M. Fisher Camp No. 319" and which stands in sharp contrast to the missing store awning under which it hangs. Many camps had individual banners that were used at local and national reunions. Each camp's flag was unique; some bore battle flags, and a foot, representing the Tar Heel, was popular on banners for North Carolina United Confederate Veterans camps. Like many camps, this one was named for a distinguished Confederate soldier from that community. Col. Charles M. Fisher was a Salisbury soldier who was killed when he was shot in the head at Manassas. These veterans also hold flags, which are of a tremendous variety, including American flags and several different versions of the Confederate flag. Using both Confederate and American flags at reunions represented reconciliation, especially as later reunions invited both Confederate and Union veterans to participate. (Rowan.)

A resident of Union County at the start of the war, John F. McCorkle enlisted in the Monroe Light Infantry, later Company B, 15th North Carolina State Troops (5th North Carolina Volunteers), on May 3, 1861. He was wounded in the hand prior to June 4, 1864, when he was hospitalized. McCorkle was paroled in Charlotte on May 3, 1865, and lies buried in Elmwood Cemetery, Mecklenburg County. (Hardy.)

Rowan County native Christian Correll was living in Union County and working as a mechanic when he enlisted in Company E, 48th North Carolina Troops, at the age of 37. Correll was wounded in the finger at Fredericksburg on December 13, 1862, and in the breast at Bristoe Station on October 14, 1863. He was captured at Hatcher's Run on October 31, 1864. He is buried in Suncrest Cemetery, Union County. (Hardy.)

Many reunions involved meals, and these veterans in Ansonville appear to be enjoying a fine repast. The setting was the home of honorary general William A. Smith, who is the front corner man with the long beard, cane, and uniform. An active member of the United Confederate Veterans, Smith was a private in Company C of the 14th North Carolina Troops and was wounded at Malvern Hill, his one and only battle.

The Confederate monument in front of the Moore County Courthouse in Carthage obviously predates modern roads in the county, since the street in front of the courthouse is unpaved in this image. The obelisk, similar in style to the Washington Monument, is an appropriate complement to the impressive edifice of the courthouse. It is flanked by cannons and stacked cannonballs.

August 15, 1907, was the date that the citizens of Catawba County gathered in Newton for the dedication of their Confederate monument. Located on the grounds of the county courthouse, the memorial is dedicated to the Confederate soldiers of the county. Many of those soldiers served in the 12th, 23rd, 28th, 32nd, 38th, 46th, 49th, 57th, and 72nd North Carolina Regiments. The inscription on the monument reads: "Confederate Heroes / No Braver Bled / For Brighter Land / Nor Brighter Land / Had A Cause So Grand." Located beside of the monument is a large seacoast cannon, a replacement for another cannon that never arrived. Another memorial lies adjacent to the 1907 monument, this one much more recent. A brass plaque includes all of the names of Catawba County soldiers killed during the war. (Hardy.)

ERECTED IN 1930 BY THE PEE DEE GUARDS
CHAPTER OF THE UNITED DAUGHTERS
OF THE CONFEDERACY OF RICHMOND
COUNTY, IN LOVING MEMORY OF OUR
CONFEDERATE SOLDIERS.

Made of Windsboro marble, the monument on the grounds of the courthouse in Rockingham, Richmond County, was dedicated on November 14, 1930, at 11:00 a.m. The march from the old Courthouse Square to the monument was led by veterans from World War I and local Boy Scouts. Former governor Cameron Morrison delivered the address, followed by the unveiling by five-year-old Ridson Thomas Nichols Jr., a descendant of one of the first volunteers from Richmond County. One side of the monument bears the inscription: "To Our Confederate Dead" while the opposite side reads "Lest We Forget." Unlike other monuments, which have a tall shaft with a bronze soldier, this simple monument has a carved Confederate battle flag, an image that would have been impossible to place on a stone in the days of Reconstruction. (SM.)

This pre-1900 photograph from Cabarrus County includes participants from a reunion of Company A of the 52nd North Carolina Troops. Like many Confederate veterans seeking to promote the spirit of reconciliation, these gentlemen pose beneath an American flag. When a reunion photograph was taken, each man generally received a copy and often identified those whose names he recalled by writing them onto the image. (Cabarrus.)

In 1929, Charlotte hosted North Carolina's only national United Confederate Veterans Reunion. Attendees included F. M. Redd (left) and Gen. Colton Lynes, who are here accompanied by ladies, including members of the United Daughters of the Confederacy wearing reunion ribbons. General Lynes, from Marietta, Georgia, served as the inspector general for the national Sons of Confederate Veterans. He was not an actual general in the Confederate army. (Charlotte.)

Simeon A. Baldwin, a private in Company A, 1st Battalion North Carolina Heavy Artillery, lived in Cumberland County at the start of the war and enlisted in New Hanover County. He was detailed as a clerk in January 1864 and served in the Commissary Department. He is buried in the Antioch Presbyterian Church Cemetery, Hoke County. (Hardy.)

Third Lt. John W. McGregor was from Anson County and enlisted in Company C, 14th North Carolina Troops (4th North Carolina Volunteers) on April 22, 1861. He worked his way through the ranks to become an officer prior to being wounded (for the third time) at Appomattox Court House. He was a "'recklessly brave officer" and is buried at East View Cemetery, Anson County. (Hardy.)

It is believed that this second national flag, carried by the 13th North Carolina State Troops, was manufactured in England and shipped through the blockade. The flag was captured by Sgt. Stephen Wrought, Company A, 141st Pennsylvania, on May 6, 1864, during the Battle of the Wilderness. The flag received the War Department number of 123. This flag was returned to North Carolina on March 25, 1905. (SM.)

It is likely that James Archibald Smith served as a private in Company D, 1st Battalion North Carolina Heavy Artillery, enlisting at the age of 17 on April 16, 1864. Smith was wounded and captured during the Battle of Fort Fisher on January 15, 1865. He is buried in the Antioch Presbyterian Church Cemetery, Hoke County. (Hardy.)

In 1910, a group of veterans gathered in Richmond County, at the community of Ellerbe Springs, which in 1861 was the site from which the "Scotch Boys" and "Pee Dee Guards" marched off to join other companies in Confederate service. Only a handful of the men in the picture have been identified. One of the gentlemen, a Captain Ingram, apparently found a wife after the war by running an advertisement. (Richmond.)

"We care not whence they came / Dear in their lifeless clay, / Whether unknown or Known to fame, / Their cause and country still the same, / They died and wore the Gray" is just one of the many inscriptions found on the monument in Laurinsburg, Scotland County. Dedicated in October 1910, the monument was made possible through the work of the Scotland Chapter of the UDC. (Hardy.)

The Fourth of July celebrations in Monroe, Union County, were "grand and glorious" in 1910. That year, the Monroe Chapter of the United Daughters of the Confederacy dedicated a monument on the grounds of the courthouse. A parade with floats opened the festivities. Then came the unveiling ceremony. According to a local newspaper: "The Old Soldiers, clad in their suits of gray and many of them wearing on their breast the crosses of honor, were present in large numbers. . . . A platform had been built and decorated on the west side of the courthouse. On this platform were seated the officers of the Union County regiments, ladies who [were] chairman of the various committees of the U.D.C. and speakers of the occasion." The Honorable T. Walker Bickett entertained the crowd with "rhetorical perfection." Following the festivities, the old soldiers, estimated to be about 150 in number, were served dinner at the Masonic Hall. (Hardy.)

These seven veterans were members of the "Anson Guards," which became Company C of the 14th North Carolina Infantry. From left to right are (first row) Thomas J. Watkins, William A. Smith, Risden T. Bennett, and E. F. Fenton; (second row) Rev. John J. McLendon, T. W. Morrison, and C. C. Bowman. (Edwards.)

John Fisher served in Company A, 42nd North Carolina Troops, from March 19, 1862, until his discharge on May 26, 1863. His fall from a horse, in which he fractured his cranium, was the reason for his discharge. Fisher is buried in the Salisbury City Cemetery, Rowan County. (Hardy.)

Mt. Zion United Methodist Church, located in Cornelius, Mecklenburg County, became an established gathering place for annual Confederate reunions. This monument, with a granite Confederate soldier on top, was dedicated in front of the church in August 1910. The cemetery that resides behind the church holds the remains of 45 veterans awaiting "the final trumpet call." (Hardy.)

This image depicts the dedication of the Confederate monument in Newton on August 15, 1907. The dedication of a Confederate monument was a cause for community celebration, drawing individuals from across the county and, if rail service was available, from across the state, reuniting them with old comrades they had not seen in years. (SA.)

William Riley Chapman, born in Cleveland County, enlisted in Company F, 55th North Carolina Troops. He was absent sick and later deserted. Chapman was apprehended, tried, and imprisoned in Salisbury. He was released from his confinement on or about December 1, 1864, and is buried in the Bethel Baptist Church, Lincoln County. (Hardy.)

This beautiful stone in the Elmwood Cemetery in Charlotte is a re-creation of the original, which was broken. The Sons of Confederate Veterans camp that bears his name had this version made and placed over the grave of Maj. Egbert B. Ross, who was mortally wounded at Gettysburg on July 1, 1863. (Hardy.)

These Ramseur, North Carolina, veterans gathered in the first decade of the 20th century to celebrate the birthday of Capt. Y. M. C. Johnson. Pictured from left to right are Y. M. C. Johnson, John Turner, "Uncle" Daniel Burgess, A. B. Covington, "Uncle" Bob McIntire, and Murphy Burrus. (SM.)

A shoemaker in Rowan County at the start of the war, William C. Ennis enlisted on July 7, 1862. He was mustered in as a private in Company K, 57th North Carolina Troops. He was in various hospitals throughout the war, suffering from typhoid fever, rubeola, and chronic diarrhea. He surrendered at Appomattox Court House and took the Oath of Allegiance in Salisbury. He is buried in the Salisbury City Cemetery, Rowan County. (Hardy.)

Born in Lincoln County in 1837, Stephen D. Ramseur was a graduate of West Point. He served as colonel of the 49th North Carolina Troops and, on November 1, 1862, was promoted to brigadier general. He was wounded four times during the war, the last at Cedar Creek, Virginia, proving fatal. He died on October 20, 1864, and is interred in the St. Luke's Episcopal Church Cemetery, Lincolnton. (Hardy.)

These Catawba County veterans are unusual in that they are wearing their hats for the photograph. Most soldiers would "uncover" for the reunion photographs. Some of the gentlemen wear reunion ribbons or badges. Catawba County alone sent over 600 men into the Confederate army.

Undoubtedly one of the most beautiful monuments in the South, this Salisbury sculpture was dedicated on June 10, 1909. It was made possible through the work of the Robert F. Hoke Chapter of the United Daughters of the Confederacy and was designed by the famous W. F. Reicksthul of New York. The bronze monument depicts a dying Confederate soldier being supported and crowned by Fame. The bronze figures rest on a pink polished granite base. The monument was crafted in Belgium and in 1909 cost $10,000. Mrs. Frances Fisher, better known as Christian Reid and as the author of *Land of the Sky*, wrote and presented a play called *Under the Southern Cross* in an effort to raise the necessary founds. The Honorable John S. Henderson was master of ceremonies on dedication day, and numerous veterans were present. The widow of Stonewall Jackson came from her home in Charlotte to attend the dedication. (SM.)

In August 1898, members of Company K of the 56th North Carolina Troops gathered in Mecklenburg County. From left to right are (first row) M. A. Emmerson, W. D. Barnhardt, Robert S. Templeton, B. D. Brown, Jon Kennerly, W. T. Cashion, John Johnston, Calvin Deweese, S. R. Andrews, and Joseph Bell; (second row) John Martin, Samuel Lowrance, Albertus Kennerly, H. J. Washam, Walter Craven, Richard Stough, Andrew Alexander, Wallace Lowrance, Allison Christenbury, and Isaac Barnett. (Archer.)

After remarks by Chief Justice Walter Clark, the veterans who attended the dedication of the Confederate monument on the grounds of the Rockingham County Courthouse were treated to a picnic. The monument, with a Mount Airy granite shaft and topped with a bronze Confederate soldier at parade rest, was dedicated on September 11, 1911. (Hardy.)

Joseph Miller lived in Cabarrus County in 1863 when, at the age of 32, he enlisted in Company A, 52nd North Carolina Troops. His date of enlistment was April 6, 1863. He was captured two months later during the Battle of Gettysburg, Pennsylvania, where he died on or about July 21, 1863, presumably of wounds. This marker, erected by his descendants, stands in Cabarrus County. (Hardy.)

Maj. Harvey Bingham was born in Watauga County in 1839. A prewar lawyer, he enlisted in September 1861 and was appointed lieutenant that same year. He was wounded in the head at the Second Battle of Manassas. After resigning, he became major of the 11th Battalion of the North Carolina Home Guard. He died in 1895 and is buried in Oakwood Cemetery in Statesville.

A grand celebration was held on May 10, 1905, at the unveiling of the Confederate monument on the grounds of the Iredell County Courthouse in Statesville. Gov. Robert B. Glenn gave an address to thousands, including 12 Confederate veterans who had received crosses of honor from the United Daughters of the Confederacy. Eight young ladies unveiled the monument, and County Commissioner L. C. Caldwell accepted the monument on behalf of the citizens of Iredell County. After reading the inscription on the monument, Caldwell turned and addressed the audience: "In the name of the ladies I present to you one of the most beautiful, most lasting tributes ever erected in North Carolina." Following the unveiling, the body moved en masse to the cemetery, where the graves of the Confederate dead were decorated. Then the old soldiers proceeded to the opera house, where a dinner was prepared for the scores of veterans who had turned out that day. (Archer.)

Three

NORTHERN PIEDMONT

The counties in the Northern Piedmont section of the Old North State witnessed the opening and closing of the war. From Raleigh, in Wake County, Gov. John W. Ellis received Abraham Lincoln's telegram requesting troops to go into the Deep South states to crush the rebellion. Ellis replied that Lincoln could get no troops from North Carolina, and on May 20, 1861, convention delegates meeting in Raleigh voted unanimously to leave the Union. Large training camps were established in Raleigh and High Point, attempting to equip and train almost 125,000 volunteers and conscripts who would serve in the Confederate forces. It was from Raleigh that young Zebulon Baird Vance, former Confederate colonel and governor after 1862, managed affairs with a skillful hand. And it was in Durham, at the Bennett Place, that Confederate general Joseph E. Johnston met federal commander William T. Sherman and surrendered the remnants of the Confederate Army of Tennessee, ending the war in the states east of the Mississippi River. In 1867, the first Decoration Day was held in Raleigh. Monuments to Confederate heroes dot the capitol grounds, and Oakwood Cemetery has more Confederate graves than any other cemetery in the state. This cemetery has not only the graves of soldiers who died in Raleigh during the war, but also the reinterred North Carolina Confederate dead from Gettysburg, Pennsylvania, and Arlington National Cemetery.

For countless years after the end of Reconstruction, the proud Confederate veterans used every opportunity to march. They marched in their own reunion parades, in monument dedications, and in Fourth of July celebrations. Here a group of veterans (possibly both Confederate and Union), are marching in a parade in Durham, honoring veterans just returned from fighting in the Great War (World War I). (SA.)

October 20, 1909, was a day of celebration in Oxford, Granville County. That day, a monument was dedicated to the Granville County Confederate dead. Gov. William Kitchin was present, along with the Granville Grays Chapter of the United Daughters of the Confederacy, a battalion of cadets from Horner's Military School, the Oxford Fire Department, Confederate veterans, and, according to one witness, "thousands of beautiful women . . . handsome men . . . and as many of God's sweetest smiles—numberless happy-faced children." (SA.)

Decoration Day, the original name of Confederate Memorial Day, has been held across the Tar Heel State since 1867. On May 10, it is customary to place flags and flowers on the graves of veterans and their spouses, much like these people are doing in Forsyth County. (Forsyth.)

Alfred Moore Scales served North Carolina as a congressional representative before the war. Enlisting as a private, he was quickly elected captain of Company H, 13th NCT, and soon became the regiment's colonel. He was wounded at Chancellorsville and again at Gettysburg, shortly after his promotion to brigadier general. After the war, he served as legislator, congressman, and governor. Upon his death in 1892, he was laid to rest in Greensboro's Green Hill Cemetery. (Hardy.)

Nothing gave old soldiers more delight than to gather for reunions. Sometimes the reunions were local affairs, with men from their own community, or possibly a regimental reunion. At other times, the reunions were statewide or national affairs. Here a group of men gather in Person County on an unknown date. (SA.)

Numerous Confederate monuments ring the grounds of the state capitol in Raleigh. The Confederate soldier monument was built under the auspices of the Raleigh Memorial Association in 1895. The shaft of the monument is 75 feet tall, with a Confederate infantryman on the top. Two lower figures include an artilleryman and cavalry troops. The monument was unveiled by one of Stonewall Jackson's granddaughters. (Hardy.)

Standing proud, with a blanket roll over his shoulder, this Confederate statue keeps watch over the town of Winston-Salem, Forsyth County. He was unveiled on October 3, 1905. There were four different speakers that day, including Mayor O. B. Eaton and Lt. Gov. Francis D. Winston. After the unveiling, the band played "Dixie," to the delight of the crowd. (Forsyth.)

Marked by a cenotaph in the churchyard at First Baptist Church in Yanceyville, Caswell County, John A. Graves made the ultimate sacrifice when he died of disease in the prison camp at Johnston's Island, Ohio. The carving on the gravestone tells us that Graves was a Mason, and the iron cross in front of his grave honors his Confederate service. (Hardy.)

Robert W. Anderson was born in 1838, attended the University of North Carolina, and was teaching Greek at his alma mater before enlisting in the 3rd North Carolina Artillery. He was an aide to his brother, Gen. George B. Anderson, until July 16, 1863, when he transferred to the staff of John Cooke. Anderson was killed on May 5, 1864, in the Battle of the Wilderness and is interred in the St. Matthew's Churchyard, Orange County. (Hardy.)

Residing in Wake County and working as a machinist, Marion Smith enlisted at the age of 21 on May 21, 1861, in Company K, 14th North Carolina State Troops (4th North Carolina Volunteers). Smith, promoted to sergeant March–June 1862, was killed during the Battle of Malvern Hill, Virginia, on July 1, 1862. This memorial stone is found in Oakwood Cemetery, Wake County. (Hardy.)

In 1890, the Wake County Ladies Memorial Association and the groups of Confederate Veterans opened a home for former Confederate soldiers in Raleigh. In this photograph, taken on May 14, 1938, are residents of the home, from left to right: William Wish, Thomas S. Arthur, William Holcomb, W. T. Mangum, and Walter Barfield. (SM.)

Vance County Court House
and Confederate Monument,
Henderson, N. C.

Schoolchildren and teachers, members of the UDC, 150 Confederate veterans, and others all gathered on November 10, 1910, to dedicate the Confederate monument in Henderson, Vance County. Speakers included Gov. William Kitchin. The monument, pictured here in an early postcard, is 35 feet tall, with a bronze soldier on the top. (Hardy.)

This great-coated Confederate soldier stands guard over the graves of 300 unidentified Southern soldiers in the Green Hill Cemetery in Greensboro. The monument was erected *c.* 1888 by the Memorial Association, precursor to the United Daughters of the Confederacy. The inscription reads: "Our Confederate Dead 1861—Dedicated to the memory of 300 unknown soldiers by the Ladies Memorial Assoc. of Greensboro, N.C." The bottom plaque commemorates a 1944 refurbishment. (Hardy.)

Court House and Confederate Monument, Warrenton, North Carolina

An early-20th-century postcard from Warrenton portrays the Confederate monument on the Warren County courthouse lawn. The bronze soldier with rifle, blanket roll, and canteen stands atop the memorial; the base is inscribed "Our Heroes" and includes carved cannonballs on the corners. The statue, erected to the memory of Warren County's Confederates, was unveiled by Annie Bell Alston in ceremonies that also included a speech by the governor and other officials. (Hardy.)

Here a group of Confederates have gathered for participation in a veterans' parade in Littleton, Warren County. The band appears to be the Lawrence O'Bryan Branch Drum and Fife Corps. The gentleman beside the driver of the carriage of ladies is holding a Tar Heel Confederate Veteran banner. (SA.)

A bronze sculpture of a matron reading to a young boy honors all North Carolina women and their sacrifices. On the sides on the monument, which stands in Raleigh's Capitol Square, bronze plaques depict loved ones bidding soldiers farewell and bringing home the dead and wounded. The monument was funded by Ashley Horne, who died before its installation in 1914. The design was by Belle Kinney. (SA.)

The oldest veterans attending the 1930 statewide veterans' reunion in Winston-Salem included, from left to right, I. A. Cowan of Winston-Salem, W. C. Meadows of Poors Knob, A. J. White of Walnut Cove, J. A. Lisk of Mount Gilead, John F. Hatley, J. M. Story of Burlington, D. E. Honeycutt of Albermarle, C. S. Holton of Charlotte, Mrs. D. E. Honeycutt, S. S. May of Yadkinville, G. H. Hall of Red Springs, and M. J. Short of Waxhall. (Forsyth.)

In this 1905 photograph, Pres. Theodore Roosevelt, while on a visit to Raleigh, Wake County, stands and salutes the North Carolina Confederate Monument as his carriage passes by. One of the gentlemen walking besides the carriage is also saluting. A year later, Roosevelt, to help with reconciliation between the North and South, endorsed the idea of a monument to Confederate dead at Arlington. (SM.)

This monument, erected in 1912 and located in Chapel Hill, Durham County, honors the students from the University of North Carolina. The lower bronze portrays the goddess of war giving a student a sword. The monument, featuring a soldier on top known as "Silent Sam," was designed by Canadian sculptor John Wilson. The bronze panel on the reverse of the monument lists students from the university who served in the Confederacy. (Hardy.)

Rising through the ranks to become captain of Company G, 2nd North Carolina Cavalry (19th North Carolina State Troops), George Pettigrew Bryan was wounded and captured on June 21, 1863, at Upperville, Virginia. His service record states that he was "killed in action" on August 16, 1864, but does not give a locality. Bryan is buried in Oakwood Cemetery, Wake County (Hardy.)

Granville County was established in 1746 and sent approximately 1,600 men to serve in the Confederate army. In this undated photograph, a large group of veterans are in formation in front of the Granville courthouse in Oxford. They are proudly displaying their third national Confederate flag. (SA.)

In September 1905, thousands gathered for the unveiling of the Confederate monument in Lexington, Davidson County. Iron crosses were presented to the veterans who were present, and a dinner was served. The monument was originally located in the center of the street, but in the 1950s, the monument was moved to the corner, still across from the courthouse. (Hardy.)

Zebulon Baird Vance was one of North Carolina's most beloved statesmen and soldiers. In honor of his service to the Old North State, this bronze statue of Vance recounting his service as a state legislator, congressman, Confederate colonel, U.S. senator, and governor, was erected in 1900 on the courthouse grounds in Raleigh, Wake County. (SM.)

Person County was named for Thomas Person, an important figure in the American Revolution but an ardent supporter of his state and an opponent to a federal union. One hundred years after his death, soldiers who had fought against just such a powerful federal government gathered in his namesake county. In this early-20th-century reunion photograph, veterans pose in front of the Person County Courthouse, and several appear to be accompanied by their wives.

Born in 1827 near Manson in Warren County, Orren Randolph Smith moved to Louisburg, Franklin County, when a teenager. He served during the Mexican War and later with Albert Sidney Johnston in suppressing the Mormons. When war came again, he enlisted in Company B, 2nd Battalion, North Carolina Troops, but was injured while on leave. Smith was appointed a quartermaster and, with the rank of major, was assigned to Marion, South Carolina. Long after the war, Smith made the claim that he had designed the "Stars and Bars," the first flag of the Confederacy. Smith also claimed that he raised this flag on the grounds of the courthouse in Louisburg, North Carolina, on March 18, 1861. Many believe that the credit of designing the "Stars and Bars" goes to Alabama resident Nicola Marschall. The dispute between these two men and their supporters remains unsolved. Smith died on March 3, 1919, and is buried in Elmwood Cemetery, Henderson, Vance County. A monument to Smith is located at the Westminster of the South in Fletcher, Henderson County. (SM.)

Many veterans, and their families, chose to remember their service to their beloved Confederacy by engraving flags on their gravestones. A variety of styles can be seen, from furled to flowing in the breeze, from battle flags to Confederate national flags. Even veterans like Jacok B. Sanders, who died 50 years after his Confederate service, still sought to pay tribute to the army in which he served as a teenager. (Forsyth.)

Gen. Lawrence O'Bryan Branch rests beneath this obelisk in Raleigh's Old City Cemetery. Branch, a prewar lawyer and statesman, served as colonel of the 33rd North Carolina before being promoted to brigadier general in November 1861. He commanded troops at New Bern, Hanover, Seven Days, and Second Manassas. At Sharpsburg, he was killed by a sharpshooter. After Branch's death, his widow, Nancy, became an integral figure in memorial and reinterment efforts. (Hardy.)

James Augustus Graham was a student in Orange County when the war came. He enlisted, at the age of 20, on April 20, 1861, in Company G, 27th North Carolina Troops. Captain Graham was twice wounded during the war and, on April 9, 1865, surrendered at Appomattox Court House, one of the few to surrender who had fought the entire war. He is buried at St. Matthews Cemetery, Orange County. (Hardy.)

A native of Augusta, Georgia, William Robertson Boggs was a West Point graduate. He served under Gen. P. T. G. Beauregard during the Battle of Fort Sumter. On November 4, 1862, Boggs was commissioned a brigadier general and fought out West. Boggs retired to North Carolina in 1911 and is buried in Old Salem Cemetery, Forsyth County. (Hardy.)

On June 29, 1910, the Reidsville Confederate monument was dedicated in a lavish ceremony that included a parade and several distinguished speakers. Some of the inscriptions read: "At their Country's Call they sprang to her defense; / And on the Altar of Civil Liberties offered as a Sacrifice / Their Property and Their Lives" and "Let Posterity / Learn Their True Story and Forever Honor / Their Patriotic Devotion." (Hardy.)

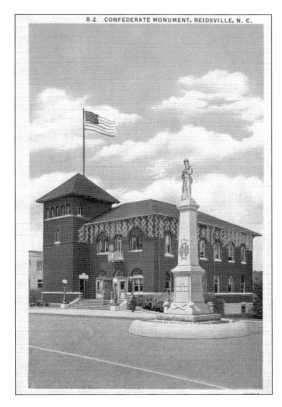

The Boy Scouts were often connected with veteran reunions. L. C. Wilkerson, pictured here on the left, organized North Carolina's first Boy Scout Troop on September 30, 1910, only six months after the movement was first founded in the United States. He and his scouts attended many reunions to provide assistance to the veterans. He is joined by N. M. Bernhardt of Rockwell, a 90-year-old veteran from Mississippi, in this 1930 image. (Forsyth.)

These six elderly soldiers gather for a 1920s reunion in Littleton, North Carolina. As the 20th century entered its second decade, numbers at reunions began to dwindle as the former Confederates passed across the river to join their former comrades. The third gentleman from the right wears both an iron cross and a reunion ribbon. Several of the others have reunion ribbons as well. (SA.)

The Confederate monument at the state capitol in Raleigh is here admired by onlookers on Hillsboro Street shortly after it was unveiled in May 1895. The monument was built under the direction of the Raleigh Memorial Association at a cost of $25,000 and was presented by the U.S. War Department in 1902. (SA.)

This group celebrates Confederate Memorial, or Decoration, Day in the Old Salem Cemetery in Winston-Salem. The graves are decorated both with flowers and Confederate flags. A brass band was part of the ceremonies, as seen at left. Contemporary soldiers can be seen at the rear of the crowd. Many decoration celebrations and monument dedications included music, military personnel, and children, like this one. (Forsyth.)

On Thursday, November 8, 1923, more than 3,000 people gathered at the Bennett Place to dedicate a monument commemorating the end of the Civil War. Fifty-eight years earlier, Confederate general Joseph Johnston surrendered his forces to federal commander William T. Sherman at this site in Durham County. (SA.)

After the war, grieving family members desperately sought to find the final resting places of their fallen Confederate loved ones. A few families were successful, largely through the diligence of the dead man's comrades, who marked his grave as best they could and reported its location to family and friends. However, countless other fathers, sons, and brothers lay in unmarked graves or mass burial trenches. When North Carolina soldiers' bodies were moved from battlefields such as Gettysburg or Chancellorsville to soldiers' sections in cemeteries like this one in Oakwood Cemetery, Raleigh, they returned to their native soil, but their individual identities remain a mystery. Identified only as a North Carolinian, this soldier's name and life story are lost to the ages. Despite the epitaph's reassurance, his mother, and thousands like her, never knew where their sons finally lay. (Hardy.)

Maj. Gen. W. A. Smith of Ansonville, the commander of the North Carolina Division of the United Confederate Veterans (seated), along with his wife, participated in this reunion with veterans in Winston-Salem in September 1930. From left to right are S. B. Carlisle of Littleton, W. S. Grissom of Gaston County, Capt. N. W. Bernhardt of Rockwell, J. A. McAskill of Hamlet, M. D. McNeill of Red Springs, T. N. Alexander of Charlotte, W. G. Johnson of Raeford, J. H. Shore of Yadkinville, and W. M. Barwick of Craven County. (Forsyth.)

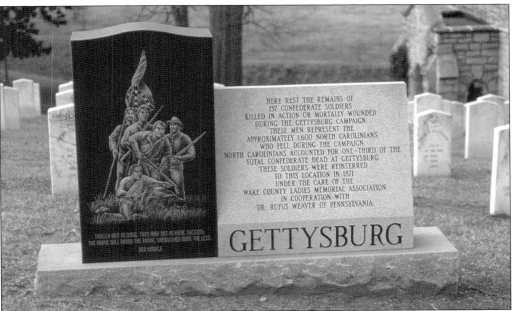

The proper burial of Confederate soldiers who were killed on battlefields or who died in hospitals became a top priority after the war. The Wake County Memorial Association led the way in North Carolina. Made up mostly of ladies, they received the remains of identified North Carolinians from Gettysburg and had them reinterred in Oakwood Cemetery in Raleigh. This marker in the cemetery commemorates their work. (Hardy.)

Taken in 1920, this photograph shows family and friends at the old soldiers' home in Raleigh. Standing in the center of the photograph are Julian S. Carr, of the 3rd North Carolina Cavalry (left), and Captain Cathey, likely James M. Cathey of Company F, 25th North Carolina Troops (right). (SM.)

This group of veterans, believed to be from Nash County, is standing in front of a monument on the capital grounds in Raleigh, Wake County. The monument is to Henry Wyatt, who enlisted in Company A, 1st North Carolina Volunteers, and was killed at the Battle of Big Bethel, Virginia, on June 10, 1861, becoming the first Confederate soldier to die in battle. (SA.)

After the passage of the Conscription Act of 1862, all men between the ages of 18 and 35 had to serve in the army unless exempt. One solution, if the conscript could afford it, was to hire a substitute. Ambros Stewart, a Forsyth County native and a 17-year-old carpenter, was hired as a substitute and enlisted on March 22, 1862, in Company K, 45th North Carolina Troops. He was a musician and was paroled in Greensboro on May 11, 1865. He is buried in the Oak Ridge United Methodist Church Cemetery, Guilford County. (Hardy.)

Col. John Randolph Lane, of the 26th North Carolina, was promoted to lieutenant colonel in October 1862. At Gettysburg, Lane seized the regiment's colors, leading his regiment through the federal lines, and was shot in the back of the head as he turned to rally his men. He survived his wounds, dying on December 31, 1908; he is buried in the Brush Creek Baptist Church Cemetery, Chatham County. (Chatham.)

The Lawrence O'Bryan Branch Drum and Fife Corps in 1909 included, from left to right, A. H. Haynes, James J. Lewis, Wiley T. Johnson, and W. D. Smith. Music was the lifeblood of a soldier. It woke him up in the morning, paraded him around the drill field, and soothed him to sleep at night. The music that ruled the soldier's life came from the drum and fife, the bugle or brass band, and the simple chords of a fiddle or banjo at night around the campfire. Once the war had ended, the soldiers who drummed and blew continued, and veteran bands played together for many decades. After the old soldiers became too feeble to play, younger men picked up the challenge, and it would be rare to find a reunion without a drum and fife corps or cornet band to provide military airs for the assembled crowd. (SM.)

Four

COASTAL PLAIN

The coastal plain of North Carolina, running east of modern-day Interstate 95, witnessed the lion's share of activity in the state during the war. Coastal fortifications south of Wilmington and at Bogue Sound and the arsenal at Fayetteville fell to North Carolina troops after the capitulation of Fort Sumter. By early 1862, the Outer Banks were back under federal control, and New Bern fell to Union forces on March 14, 1862. There were numerous attempts to recapture the coastal towns of New Bern and Plymouth, some more successful than others. In March 1865, a federal army approached from the south, and two of the last large-scale land battles of the war were fought in Averasboro and Bentonville. The forts at Wilmington also fell in early 1865, and with the capture of Wilmington on February 22, 1865, the last major seaport of the Confederacy was closed. Following the war, the citizens of Fayetteville were the first in the Tar Heel State to erect a monument to the fallen Confederate soldiers. Some of the most beautiful cemeteries in the state, with ornate grave markers and beautiful stones, lie in the vicinity of Fayetteville and Wilmington. The area also has the most Civil War–related parks in the state, including Forts Anderson and Fisher south of Wilmington, Fort Macon at Morehead, Fort Branch near Hamilton, and the Bentonville Battlefield State Park.

In 1911 or 1912, these New Hanover County veterans met in Wilmington. They are, from left to right (first row) two unidentified, Richard M. V. Reaves, Dr. William Dougald MacMillan, Benjamin Franklin Hall, and two unidentified; (second row) unidentified, ? Skipper, unidentified, Henry Kuhl, and unidentified; (third row) Rev. Andrew J. Howell, three unidentified, either Dr. William Baldwin (dentist) or Dr. ? Talleway, two unidentified, and Edgar Williams. (Cape Fear.)

Built for John and Amy Harper, this c. 1885 Greek Revival farmhouse served as a field hospital for Sherman's 14th Corps during the Battle of Bentonville in March 1865. Over 500 soldiers, including almost 50 Confederates, were treated in the house or on the grounds. Today the site is preserved as part of the Bentonville Battleground State Park. (Hardy.)

Just a few days after the close of the war, a group of ladies secured from the mayor of Fayetteville a section of the Cross Creek Cemetery in which 18 Confederate soldiers were already buried. Twelve others were brought from other sites and interred. It was decided that a monument was needed to mark the spot, and a Ladies Memorial Association was established. A silk quilt was made by some local ladies, and shares in the work were sold for $1 each. Once the $300 was raised for the monument, the ladies employed George Lauder of Fayetteville to manufacture and raise the marker. The monument, dedicated December 30, 1868, bears this inscription: "Nor shall your glory be forgot / While fame her record keeps / Or honor points the hallowed spot / Where valor proudly sleeps. . . . / On fame's eternal camping ground / Their silent tents are spread / Rest on embalmed and sainted dead / Dear as the blood ye gave." This monument, the fifth erected in the South following the war, originally had a cross on the top. (Hardy.)

Members of Company E of the 20th Regiment North Carolina Troops are here seen in an undated photograph at Calypso, North Carolina. The company was originally organized at Faison, North Carolina, on April 16, 1861, six weeks before the state formally seceded from the Union. (SA.)

On May 10, 1920, young boys and old soldiers, including one with his reunion ribbons, gather at the monument at Southwest Creek near Kinston. The boys are Robert Hoke Webb and Robert Hoke Pollard, grandsons of Maj. Gen. Robert F. Hoke, the victorious Confederate commander of the Battle of Southwest Creek. An eagle-topped bronze plaque describes the March 6, 1865, action. (SM.)

Nathaniel Harding was born in 1847 in Beaufort County. He enlisted as a private in Company I, 67th North Carolina Troops, also known as Whitford's Battalion North Carolina Partisan Rangers. A family story relates that his life was saved by a Union officer who rescued him from drowning when the heavily-laden Harding fell into a creek during battle. This gentleman apparently had a powerful influence on Harding and may have influenced his choice of postwar education. Following his service, Harding attended Trinity College in Hartford, Connecticut, and was also ordained a priest in the Episcopal Church, serving at St. Peter's Church in Washington, North Carolina. He was an active and beloved minister who helped shape his parish into one of the strongest in the state and who took part in the educational leadership of the county. Harding, pictured here proudly wearing his iron cross, died on June 27, 1917, and is buried at Oakdale Cemetery in Washington. (Harding.)

This early linen postcard shows the Confederate monument in Elizabeth City, Pasquotank County. The monument was dedicated on May 10, 1911, and was erected by the D. H. Hill Chapter of the United Daughters of the Confederacy. The inscription reads: "1861–1865 'Our Heroes' To our Confederate dead. Erected by the D. H. Hill Chapter United Daughters of the Confederacy, Elizabeth City, N.C. May 19th, 1911." (Hardy.)

William Proudfoot Wemyss was 29 years old when he enlisted in Cumberland County on September 2, 1863. He was appointed captain of Company D, 2nd Battalion North Carolina Local Defense Troops. He lies buried in Cross Creek Cemetery, Cumberland County. (Hardy.)

Born in New Hanover County, Gaston Mears was colonel of the 3rd North Carolina State Troops. He was killed on July 1, 1862, during the Battle of Malvern Hill, Virginia, and is buried in Oakdale Cemetery, New Hanover County. (Hardy.)

Six of Nash County's veterans stand on the steps of the YMCA in Nashville. The gentleman on the right wears an iron cross on his left lapel and a reunion ribbon on his right. Three of the gentlemen have their names written on the image. (SA.)

In 1904, the Bell Battery Chapter of the United Daughters of the Confederacy erected this 30-foot granite monument in front of the courthouse in Edenton. The monument is topped by a soldier equipped for battle, and the inscription reads: "Our Confederate Dead / 1861–1865 / Gashed With Honorable Scars / Low In Glory's Lap They Lie / Though They Fell Like Stars / Streaming Splendor Through The Sky." (Hardy.)

Rose O'Neal Greenhow, a Confederate spy, acquired information through her considerable charm and Washington social connections. Imprisoned in her home and in the Old Capitol Prison, Mrs. Greenhow was eventually released and traveled to Europe to rally support for the South. Upon her return, her blockade runner was attacked off the North Carolina coast; she drowned while attempting to reach shore. She was buried in Wilmington's Oakdale Cemetery with military honors; roses are still left upon her grave. (Hardy.)

The William Dorsey Pender Chapter of the United Daughters of the Confederacy dedicated a monument on October 29, 1904, on the Commons in Tarboro, Edgecombe County. This monument, containing a granite shaft and a bronze Confederate soldier at parade rest, cost $2,250. The Commons and monument were the subject of an early linen postcard. (Hardy.)

Created on February 16, 1875, Pender County was named in honor of William Dorsey Pender, a Confederate general who was wounded in the leg on the second day of the Battle of Gettysburg, Pennsylvania. Infection set in, and following an emergency amputation, Pender died on July 18, 1863. His body was returned to North Carolina and buried in the Calvary Church Cemetery in Tarboro. This early photograph shows the Confederate monument in Burgaw, which was dedicated on May 27, 1914, and which features the beloved general's image. Funds for the monument were largely raised by Point Caswell veteran Maj. R. P. Paddision, who died only six months after the monument's installation. (SM.)

These two veterans have been identified as a Major Woodhouse of Currituck County (left) and Rufus Reddick of Gates County. Mr. Reddick is wearing his iron cross. These were awarded to veterans by the United Daughters of the Confederacy. (SM.)

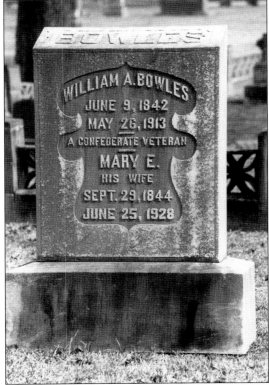

Enlisting at the age of 17 on September 2, 1863, William Alexander Bowles served first in Company C, 2nd Battalion North Carolina Local Defense Troops before transferring to Company B. This battalion was commonly referred to as the "Arsenal Guard" and was composed of employees, detailed men, and nonconscripts who worked at the Fayetteville Arsenal and Armory. Bowles is buried in the Cross Creek Cemetery, Cumberland County. (Hardy.)

This image of the Sampson County Confederate Memorial was likely taken at the monument's dedication on May 10, 1916. The monument was erected by the Ashford-Sillers Chapter of the UDC and is inscribed: "In Honor of the Confederate Soldiers of Sampson County 'Who bore the flag of a sacred trust / And fell in a cause, though lost, still just / And died for me and you / 1861 1865." (SA.)

Alexander Davis served in Company A, 31st North Carolina Troops from September 6, 1861, until September 15, 1862, when he was discharged. Records indicate that he died at a hospital in Wilmington on January 20, 1863, of pneumonia. This grave marker is located in the St. Paul's Church Cemetery, Robeson County. (Hardy.)

In the early months of 1865, Fort Fisher, off the coast of Wilmington, fell to federal forces, effectively closing off Wilmington and its port to the Confederacy. In 1866, the Confederate casualties of the battle were moved to the Confederate section of Wilmington's Oakdale Cemetery. On May 10, 1872, the Ladies Memorial Association, which later became part of Cape Fear Chapter No. 3, United Daughters of the Confederacy, dedicated the monument over the Fort Fisher graves. The monument features a life-size bronze statue modeled after a Wilmington soldier. The dapper Confederate, decked in greatcoat, boots, and jaunty kepi, has his arm resting on the musket's muzzle, a peculiar and unlikely pose. Bronze plaques with classically styled images of General Lee and Stonewall Jackson adorn the sides, and the base is inscribed "To the Confederate Dead." A flagpole behind the monument flies the Confederate national flag. (SM.)

Veterans of Company E, 20th Regiment North Carolina Troops, gather with their families at a reunion in Calypso in Duplin County in 1904. The festive occasion included music, as evidenced by the banjo player on the right. It is also interesting to note the differing fashion choices of the older, more traditional individuals and their younger counterparts. (SA.)

On Confederate Memorial Day, 1902, thousands gathered on St. James Square for the unveiling of a large Confederate monument in Fayetteville, Cumberland County. One of the inscriptions on the monument reads: "The women of Cumberland County to Confederate dead May 20th, 1861–May 10, 1902. For them shall fall the tears of a Nation's Grief." (Hardy.)

Working as a mechanic in Randolph County in 1861, David C. Lamb enlisted on June 5, 1861, in Company I, 27th North Carolina Troops. He was wounded in October 1862 and, on July 3, 1863, captured at Gettysburg. Lamb later joined the Union navy, serving on board the USS *Princeton*, USS *Pocahontas*, and USS *North Carolina*. He is buried in the Cross Creek Cemetery, Cumberland County. (Hardy.)

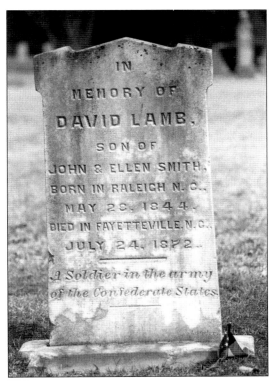

Gabriel James Boney, a Confederate soldier, died in 1915, leaving a $20,000 fund for the erection of a Confederate monument. This Wilmington statue, erected by the United Confederate Veterans and United Daughters of the Confederacy in 1924, stands at the intersection of Third and Dock Streets. The gallant bronze soldier prepares to load his musket, as the Latin inscription reads, "for altars and hearths." (Hardy.)

A young visitor to the Bentonville battlefield pays tribute to the 2,000 Confederate soldiers honored by the impressive Confederate marker. The March 1865 battle, a desperate but unsuccessful attempt by Gen. Joseph E. Johnston to defeat General Sherman's forces, bought only a few days of reprieve for the beleaguered South. (SM.)

Born in Wilmington, Robert Harper Cowan was a University of North Carolina graduate. He served in the 3rd North Carolina before being promoted to colonel of the 18th North Carolina. Resigning because of illness on November 11, 1862, Cowan went on to become a railroad president and North Carolina legislator. He is buried in Oakdale Cemetery, New Hanover County. (Hardy.)

The two last Civil War soldiers to serve in Congress were Isaac R. Sherwood (standing, left) and Charles M. Stedman (standing, right). Sherwood served as a Union general during the war and later as a U.S. representative from Ohio. Stedman, a North Carolina native, was a Confederate major. After the war, he was a U.S. representative. At the time of his death in 1930, he was the last remaining U.S. congressman to have served in the war. (SM.)

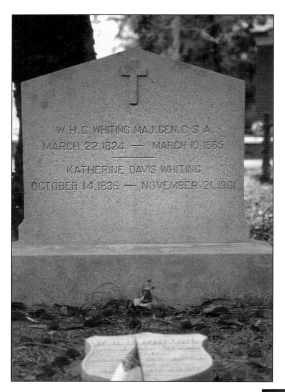

Among the many Confederate graves found in Wilmington's Oakdale Cemetery is that of Maj. Gen. William Henry Chase Whiting. Born in Mississippi, Whiting commanded in Virginia until being assigned to the defenses around Wilmington. He was mortally wounded in the right thigh and hip and captured on January 15, 1865, during the Battle of Fort Fisher; he died on March 10, 1865, at Fort Columbus, New York. (Hardy.)

Wilmington native William MacRae enlisted as a private in the Monroe Light Infantry at the beginning of the war and eventually rose to the rank of brigadier general. After the war, he became a railroad official and died February 11, 1882, in Augusta, Georgia. He is buried in Oakdale Cemetery in Wilmington, but for many years, his grave was unmarked. Only in the last years of the 20th century did he receive a proper marker. (Hardy.)

Undoubtedly the monument in Nash County was one of the most impressive markers in the state. Dedicated on May 10, 1917, the $15,000 monument was made possible through the donations of Robert H. Ricks. The monument originally contained four figures on each corner, as pictured here: an infantry soldier, artilleryman, cavalry trooper, and commanding officer, with a color bearer on top. The soldiers surrounding the bottom of the monument, made of Georgia marble, have since disappeared. The inscription on the front of the monument reads: "To the Confederate Soldiers of Nash County, who in 1861 in obedience to the summons of their state freely offered their lives, their fortunes, and their sacred honor in behalf of the cause of Constitutional Liberty and Self Government, and through four years of war so bore themselves in victory and defeat as to win the plaudits of the world and set an example of exalted and unselfish patriotism which will ever be unfailing inspiration to all future generations of American citizens."

During the war, a Confederate wayside hospital, known as General Hospital Number 2, was located in Wilson. At least 128 Confederates died at the hospital. This monument, dedicated on May 10, 1902, rests above the mound that these soldiers occupy in Maplewood Cemetery, Wilson County. The monument was made possible through the work of the Wilson County Confederate Veterans and the John W. Durham Chapter of the United Daughters of the Confederacy. (SA.)

Wilmington's George Davis served as the attorney general of the Confederacy. On April 20, 1911, the Cape Fear Chapter of the United Daughters of the Confederacy unveiled this statue in his honor at the intersection of Third and Market Streets. The granite base is inscribed: "George Davis, Senator and Attorney General of the Confederate States of America 1820–1896 / George Davis. Erected in loving memory by the United Daughters of the Confederacy / Scholar Patriot Statesman Christian." (Hardy.)

Pender County was created from portions of New Hanover County on February 16, 1875, and named in honor of Confederate general William Pender. On May 27, 1914, in Burgaw, citizens gathered to dedicate a monument to the Confederate soldiers from the area, after which a dinner was served. The monument was made possible under the auspices of the Pender County Chapter of the United Daughters of the Confederacy. (Hardy.)

On the Confederate monument in Burgaw, Pender County, is a stone relief of Maj. Gen. William Dorsey Pender, for whom the county was named. Pender, born in 1834, was mortally wounded commanding a division at the Battle of Gettysburg. He died on July 18, 1863, and is interred in the Cavalry Churchyard in Tarboro, Edgecombe County, North Carolina. (Hardy.)

The city of Wilmington contained the last port not in Union hands for the Confederacy. Through this port, countless supplies were brought in through the blockade. In January 1865, the Union attacked the defensive works, and on January 12, 1865, Fort Fisher fell and the port of Wilmington was closed. This photograph, taken c. 1930, shows a small group of people standing by the Fort Fisher monument. (SM.)

This gravestone, found in the Camp Ground United Methodist Church in Fayetteville, Cumberland County, is for J. W. Johnson, who most likely served in Company D, 3rd Battalion, North Carolina Junior Reserves. The 3rd Battalion was made up of men between the ages of 15 and 18 and saw action at the Battles of Forts Fisher and Anderson and at Bentonville. (Hardy.)

Maj. Alexander MacRae served in the 1st Battalion North Carolina Heavy Artillery. This battalion served in the Battles of Forts Fisher and Anderson in 1865. The few men left were assigned as infantry to Hagood's Brigade. Major MacRae is buried in Oakdale Cemetery in Wilmington. His son, Brig. Gen. William MacRae, is interred in the same plot. (Hardy.)

In March 1895, 30 years after the Battle of Bentonville, the Military Rifles of Goldsboro in Wayne County erected this monument approximately 300 feet from the Harper House, used as a hospital during the battle. The marker is granite with a four-foot base and six-foot shaft. A stylized minie ball tops the monument. Hundreds attended the unveiling of the monument, which also featured a "Girls Guard of Honor." (SM.)

People all across the Tar Heel State mourned the death of William Dorsey Pender. An Edgecombe County native, Pender attended West Point and fought Native Americans in the West but resigned on March 21, 1861, to cast his lot with the Confederacy. He commanded the 13th North Carolina before being promoted to brigadier general on June 3, 1862. When Robert E. Lee reorganized his army after the death of Stonewall Jackson, Pender was selected to command A. P. Hill's "Light Division." During his first battle as a division commander, Pender was wounded in the leg on July 2, 1863, at Gettysburg. On the road back to Virginia, infection set in, and the leg was amputated. Pender did not recover from the operation and died on July 18. His body was returned to North Carolina and interred in the Calvary Church in Tarboro, Edgecombe County. On April 14, 1923, the monument pictured in this photograph was dedicated. The five flags being held by the ladies all appear to be original and were probably some of the flags that the regiments in Pender's brigade or division carried during the war. (SM.)

Five

North Carolina's Tribute to Jefferson Davis

Following the cessation of hostilities, Jefferson Davis was the most widely despised man, North or South. The South placed the loss of a Southern nation entirely on the shoulders of Davis. The North considered him personally responsible for the assassination of Abraham Lincoln despite a lack of evidence in the matter. He spent time in prison following the war, time the federal government spent trying to build a case of treason against Davis for a trial that never came to fruition. After Davis's release, he made his home in Mississippi. Never convicted nor exonerated, Davis died December 6, 1889, and was first interred in the Metairie Cemetery in New Orleans. After three years, the family finally consented to have the body interred in Hollywood Cemetery in Richmond, Virginia. Richmond was the home of the Confederacy's capital, and Hollywood Cemetery was the most famous cemetery in the South. J. E. B. Stuart was buried in Hollywood, along with 25 other Confederate generals. The cemetery was also the final resting place of the Gettysburg Dead, over 2,000 soldiers reinterred from the Pennsylvania battlefield. Jefferson Davis began his final journey on May 28, 1893. Davis, the only president of the Confederate States of America, was honored in numerous cities, including New Orleans, Mobile, Montgomery, Atlanta, Greensboro, and Richmond. Though countless numbers turned out to pay their respects, Davis's widow, Varina, remained in New York during the procession's travels and met the train in Richmond for her husband's reinterment. In poor health and overcome by grief, Mrs. Davis was physically and emotionally incapable of making the journey with its many stops and constant public attention.

It took three years for the Davis family to decide upon a final resting place for the late Confederate president. They finally choose Hollywood in Richmond, Virginia. From a temporary resting place in Metairie Cemetery in New Orleans, his remains were taken to Virginia in a funeral procession that would prove to be the most elaborate in Southern history. On May 30, 1893, the train made six stops in North Carolina. In Charlotte, former Confederate major general Robert F. Hoke, a part of the North Carolina delegation to the funeral in Richmond, boarded the train, an unusual move for a man who seldom took part in any Confederate memorial activities. After a brief stop in Salisbury, the train proceeded to Greensboro, where banks and stores were closed and flags flown at half-mast. In Durham, 500 schoolchildren dropped flowers on the coffin. Finally the train reached Raleigh. (SM.)

The train reached Raleigh approximately two and a half hours late. It was a warm, sunny day, and a crowd of 20,000 had gathered to pay their respects. Confederate flags were displayed, businesses were closed and draped in black, and church bells tolled throughout the city. (SM.)

Davis's elaborate funeral carriage was driven through Raleigh by his former employee, a free black man named James J. Jones. He had served Davis in the Confederate White House and was with the president at the time of his arrest. After the war, Jones was a successful Raleigh businessman and politician. He asked for the honor of driving the funeral carriage when the procession came to Raleigh. (SM.)

Raleigh leaders created a unique carriage to transport Davis's remains from the depot to the state capitol. Inside a lavish, temple-like structure, Davis's casket rested under the battle flag of the 5th North Carolina Troops. On each corner of the carriage rode a young daughter of a North Carolina veteran, dressed in white with a black sash and carrying small versions of each of the four flags of the Confederacy. (SM.)

After leaving Raleigh, the funeral train traveled back through Durham and Greensboro, then north for a brief stop in Reidsville, where 2,000 to 3,000 people had assembled, including the 3rd Regiment of state troops. After leaving Reidsville, the train proceeded to Virginia, arriving shortly after 3:00 a.m. on March 31.

In the Raleigh capitol rotunda, the remains of Davis lay in state for two hours while nearly 5,000 filed past to pay their respects. With the accompaniment of a 75-voice choir, women, old soldiers, and others passed by the flower-covered casket before the casket was returned to the funeral train to continue its journey northward to Richmond. (SM.)

Six

OUT OF STATE

War came and drew thousands of North Carolinians from their native soil. Tar Heel military flags bore battle honors now synonymous with some of the most important actions of the war: North Carolina's sons witnessed some of the war's opening shots at Big Bethel and Manassas, charged up the slopes of Gettysburg, struggled through the tangled underbrush of Chancellorsville and the Wilderness, endured the trenches of Petersburg and Atlanta, and stood in grief as the war shuddered to a close at Durham's Station and Appomattox. Many of these Tar Heels gave their lives far from home and were buried in strange soil. While the dedicated volunteers of memorial associations managed to get some of these men moved to graves in the Old North State, many more continue to sleep in the fields where they fought and died. Some were fortunate enough to receive individual grave markers. Others are honored with more general state markers that salute the valor and sacrifice of North Carolina's men. Across the fields where these men served are scattered remembrances of the price they paid for the state they loved.

On April 10, 1905, the first Confederate monument at Appomattox Courthouse, Virginia, was unveiled by veterans. The war had been over for 40 years. In addition to the young men from the brass band, Julian S. Carr stands to the left, apparently directing the musicians. (SA.)

Henry Lawson Wyatt bears the distinction of being the first Confederate soldier killed during the Civil War. He was a Richmond, Virginia, native living in Edgecombe County when the war came, and he enlisted in Company A, 1st North Carolina Volunteers. Wyatt, who was just 19 years old, was killed on June 10, 1861, at the Battle of Big Bethel Church, Virginia. He is buried in Hollywood Cemetery, Richmond, Virginia. (Hardy.)

North Carolina sent most of her men to fight in Virginia. But a few regiments served in the western theater of the war. This monument, designed by Aristide Cianfarani and cut from Georgia granite, was dedicated in Vicksburg, Mississippi, on May 18, 1925. The 29th North Carolina Troops, the 39th North Carolina Troops, and the 60th North Carolina Troops are commemorated on the monument. (NPS.)

On October 20, 1864, North Carolina native Maj. Gen. Stephen Dodson Ramseur died of the wounds he had received in the Battle of Cedar Creek the day before. He was taken to Belle Grove House and tended by Union officers, former friends, who had his body embalmed and sent home. In 1919, the general's daughter unveiled this 25-foot marble column raised to her father's memory near the site of Belle Grove. (SM.)

Dedicated in 1965 at the conclusion of the Civil War centennial, the Confederate Soldiers and Sailors Monument depicts a Confederate soldier, with flag raised, looking back and encouraging his comrades to join him in the fight. This monument on the Gettysburg battlefield was designed by Donald Delue. All of the Southern states, including North Carolina, contributed to its funding. (SM.)

The Fredericksburg Confederate Cemetery was established by the Ladies Memorial Association. Dedicated in May 1870, the cemetery is the final resting place for 3,553 men from 14 states, many of whom are unknown; they were moved from the battlefields around Fredericksburg. One such man is Pvt. William Hartley, of Company E, 37th North Carolina Troops, who was killed on May 3, 1863, at the Battle of Chancellorsville. (Hardy.)

James McCullen was 47 years old when he enlisted in Company C, 5th North Carolina Calvary (63rd North Carolina Troops), on May 16, 1862. The Sampson County native was wounded and captured on June 19, 1863, at the Battle of Middleburg, Virginia. He was taken to the Lincoln General U.S. Army hospital, where he died on June 25, 1863. Private McCullen is buried in the Confederate section at Arlington National Cemetery, Washington, D.C. (Hardy.)

For many Confederate and Union veterans, there was a need to mark the positions their regiments fought in at battlefields around the nation. This marker, located on Snodgrass Hill at the Chickamauga, Tennessee, battlefield, denotes the position that the 58th North Carolina Troops occupied during the September 19, 1863, battle. (Hardy.)

Lincoln County native Robert Daniel Johnston was a prewar lawyer who began the war as captain of Company K, 23rd North Carolina Infantry. He served gallantly in the peninsular campaign and the Battles of Seven Pines, South Mountain, Sharpsburg, Gettysburg, and Spotsylvania, rising to the rank of brigadier general. He died in 1919, one of the last surviving Confederate generals, and is buried in Mount Hebron Cemetery in Winchester. (Hardy.)

Members of the United Daughters of the Confederacy, the United Confederate Veterans, and the North Carolina Historical Commission gather around the monument near Bunker Hill, Virginia, that honors Gen. James Johnston Pettigrew. The badly wounded Pettigrew died on July 17, 1863, at nearby Boyd House en route to Winchester after being shot at Falling Waters in the retreat from Gettysburg. Pettigrew was critical in the third day's assault against the federal forces.

Jesse Elihu Luther of Wilkes County was one of the oldest veterans in North Carolina. He is pictured here attending the 75th Gettysburg anniversary in 1938. A member of Company F of the 37th North Carolina Troops, he lived to be 102 years old with 84 great-grandchildren and 19 great-great-grandchildren before his death in May 1946.

Stephen Dodson Ramseur's brigade, composed of the 2nd, 4th, 14th, and 30th North Carolina Regiments, saw heavy action at the battle of Spotsylvania Court House, Virginia, on May 12, 1864. The brigade helped stem the tide during the federal breakthrough. This monument, erected on the battlefield in September 2001, commemorates their service. (Hardy.)

One in every four Confederate soldiers who fell during the battle of Gettysburg was from North Carolina. This monument, erected by the United Daughters of the Confederacy from North Carolina, tells of the valor of North Carolina's sons. "Their valorous deeds will be enshrined in the hearts of men long after these transient memorials have crumbled to dust" is but one of the inscriptions on the memorial. (SA.)

Gathering on April 10, 1905, at the site where in Appomattox, Virginia, Cox's North Carolina fired the last volley on the Army of Northern Virginia on April 9, 1865, a group of veterans and citizens dedicated a monument. North Carolina governor R. B. Glenn read an address to the large crowd. (SM.)

In his July 1929 address at the dedication of the North Carolina monument at Gettysburg, Gov. O. Max Gardner painted this picture: "The heroic group represents five typical North Carolina soldiers . . . [that] have just emerged from a small wooded area. . . . They suddenly see the awful struggle in front of them, the Federals are just across a small ravine, both sides of which are covered with fighting men, many of whom have been wounded. . . . The leader of the group pushed forward determined on his grim task; the younger man just behind him is stunned momentarily at the awful sight; the bearded soldier to his left, realizing what is taking place in the youth's mind draws close to him and whispers confidence. The color bearer in the rear presses forward, holding the flag aloft and well to the front of the group. At their right, one knee on the ground, is an officer encouraging his men, his presence and wounds indicating that the struggle has been in progress some time." (SM.)

BIBLIOGRAPHY

Clark, Walter, ed. *Histories of Several Regiments and Battalions from North Carolina in the Great War, 1861 to 1865*. Raleigh, NC: E. M. Uzzell, 1901.

Collins, Donald E. *The Death and Resurrection of Jefferson Davis*. New York: Rowman and Littlefield Publishers, Inc., 2005.

Cunningham, S. A., ed. *Confederate Veteran Magazine*. Nashville, TN: 1893–1932.

Dedmondt, Glenn. *The Flags of Civil War North Carolina*. Gretna, LA: Pelican Publishing Company, 2003.

Johnson, Clint. *Touring the Carolinas' Civil War Sites*. Winston-Salem, NC: John F. Blair, 1996.

Krick, Robert K. *Lee's Colonels*. Dayton, OH: Morningside Bookshop, 1979.

Manari, Louis H., and Weymouth T. Jordan, eds. *North Carolina Troops, 1861–1865*. 11 Vols. Raleigh, NC: North Carolina Department of Archives and History, 1961 to present.

Owen, Richard and James Owen. *Generals at Rest: The Grave Site of the 425 Official Confederate Generals*. Shippensburg, PA: White Main Publishing, Inc., 1997.

Powell, William S., ed. *Biographical Dictionary of North Carolina*. 6 vols. Raleigh, NC: North Carolina Department of Archives and History, 1995.

Smith, S. L. *North Carolina's Confederate Monuments and Memorials*. [n.p.]

Warner, Ezra J. *Generals in Gray: Lives of the Confederate Commanders*. Baton Rouge: Louisiana State University Press, 1959.

Mouser, Bill. "Palin and Evangelicals." No pages. Online: http://fiveaspects.net/palin-and-evangelicals/.

Niebuhr, Reinhold. "Religion: Male and Female." *Time* 75.26 (June 1960). Online: http://www.time.com/time/magazine/article/0,9171,827700,00.html.

Noren, Carol M. *The Woman in the Pulpit.* Nashville: Abingdon Press, 1992.

Parker, Kim, and Eileen Patten. "The Sandwich Generation: Rising Financial Burdens for Middle-Aged Americans." No pages. Online: http://www.pewsocialtrends.org/2013/01/30/the-sandwich-generation/.

Phillips, Rob. "Research: Millennials Are Spiritually Diverse." No pages. Online: http://www.lifeway.com/Article/LifeWay-Research-finds-American-millennials-are-spiritually-diverse.

Pierce, Ronald W., and Rebecca Merrill Groothuis, editors. *Discovering Biblical Equality: Complementarity Without Hierarchy.* Downers Grove, IL: InterVarsity Press Academic, 2005.

Piper, John, and Wayne Grudem, editors. *Recovering Biblical Manhood and Womanhood: A Response to Evangelical Feminism.* Wheaton, IL: Crossway Books, 1991.

Rainey, Russ. "Willow Creek Reveal Study: a Summary." No pages. Online: http://www.christiancoachingcenter.org/index.php/russ-rainey/coachingchurch2/.

Roberts, Sam. "51% of Women Are Now Living Without Spouse." *The New York Times* (Jan. 16, 2007). Online: http://www.nytimes.com/2007/01/16/us/16census.html.

Robinson, Haddon W. *Biblical Preaching: The Development and Delivery of Expository Messages.* Grand Rapids, MI: Baker Book House, 1980.

Robinson, Haddon, and Craig Brian Larson, editors. *The Art and Craft of Biblical Preaching: A Comprehensive Resource for Today's Communicators.* Grand Rapids, MI: Zondervan, 2005.

Saucy, Robert L. *The Church in God's Program.* Chicago: Moody Press, 1972.

Saucy, Robert L., and Judith K. TenElshof. *Women and Men in Ministry: A Complementary Perspective.* Chicago: Moody Press, 2001.

Sayers, Dorothy L. *Are Women Human? Penetrating, Sensible, and Witty Essays on the Role of Women in Society.* Grand Rapids, MI: Wm. B. Eerdmans, 1971.

Seinfeld, Jerry. "Seinfeld Talk About Public Speaking and Death," YouTube video, :13, accessed August 30, 2013, http://youtube/kL7fTLjFzAg.

Smith, Christine M. *Weaving the Sermon: Preaching in a Feminist Perspective.* Louisville, KY: Westminster/John Knox Press, 1989.

Spencer, Aída Besançon. *Beyond the Curse: Women Called to Ministry.* Peabody, MA: Hendrickson Publishers, Inc., 2000.

Spilman, Ramona Ann. "Evangelical Women in the Pulpit: Identification of Characteristics that Contribute to the Effectiveness of Evangelical Women Pursuing God's Call to Serve as Preacher and Pastor to the Local Church." PhD diss., Gordon-Conwell Seminary, 2006.

Sumner, Sarah. *Men and Women in the Church: Building Consensus on Christian Leadership.* Downers Grove, IL: InterVarsity Press, 2003.

Tannen, Deborah. *You Just Don't Understand: Women and Men in Conversation.* New York: HarperCollins Publishers, Inc., 1990.

Tertullian. "On the Apparel of Women." Translated by S. Thelwall. In *The Ante-Nicene Fathers,* vol. 4, edited by Alexander Roberts and James Donaldson. Grand Rapids, MI: Wm. B. Eerdmans, 1976.

Bibliography

Thompson, Derek, and Jordan Weissmann. "The Cheapest Generation: Why Millennials Aren't Buying Cars or Houses, and What That Means for the Economy." *The Atlantic* (Sept. 2012). Online: http://www.theatlantic.com/magazine/archive/2012/09/the-cheapest-generation/309060/2.

Torjesen, Karen Jo. *When Women Were Priests: Women's Leadership in the Early Church and the Scandal of Their Subordination in the Rise of Christianity.* New York: HarperCollins Publishers, 1993.

Vincent, Marvin R. *Word Studies in the New Testament*, Vol. 3. Peabody, MA: Hendrickson Publishers, 1954.

Vines, Jerry, and Jim Shaddix. *Power in the Pulpit: How to Prepare and Deliver Expository Sermons.* Chicago: Moody Press, 1999.

Vines, W. E. *Vines' Expository Dictionary of the New Testament.* Old Tappan, NJ: Fleming Revell Company, 1966.

Ware, Bruce. "Male and Female Complementarity and the Image of God." No pages. Online: http://www.cbmw.org/Journal/Vol-7-No-1/Male-and-Female-Complementarity-and-the-Image-of-God.

Wilhite, Keith, and Scott M. Gibson, editors. *The Big Idea of Biblical Preaching: Connecting the Bible to People.* Grand Rapids, MI: Baker Books, 1998.

Winston, George, and Dora Winston. *Recovering Biblical Ministry by Women.* Longwood, FL: Xulon Press, 2003.

Wuest, Kenneth S. *Wuest's Word Studies from the Greek New Testament*, Vol.1. Grand Rapids, MI: Wm. B. Eerdmans, 1998.

Zuck, Roy B. *Spirit-Filled Teaching: Teaching the Power of the Holy Spirit in Your Ministry.* Nashville: Thomas Nelson Publishers, 1998.